PRAISE FOR

Wildflower

"Empowering and inspirational."

—*People*

"Inspiring. . . . *Wildflower* is true to its name, sharing a story of someone who bloomed despite obstacles and dedicated herself to beauty inside and out even when doing so wasn't so simple."

—*Town & Country*

"*Wildflower* is a stunning story of grit, grace, and resilience. Aurora James takes us on a vivid journey through a life informed by creativity, vision, and an indefatigable entrepreneurial spirit while always staying grounded in her commitment to the highest principles and values. . . . A must-read!"

—HUMA ABEDIN, *New York Times* bestselling author of *Both/And*

"A very inspiring modern tale from a beautiful woman with a beautiful soul."

—DIANE VON FURSTENBERG, *New York Times* bestselling author of *The Woman I Wanted to Be*

Wildflower

a memoir

Aurora James

CROWN
NEW YORK

2024 Crown Trade Paperback Edition

Copyright © 2023 by Aurora James and Bruised Fruit, LLC
Reader's guide copyright © 2023 by Penguin Random House LLC

Published in the United States by Crown, an imprint of Crown Publishing Group,
a division of Penguin Random House LLC, New York.

Crown and the Crown colophon are registered trademarks of Penguin Random House LLC.

Originally published in the United States in hardcover and ebook by Crown, an imprint of the
Crown Publishing Group, a division of Penguin Random House LLC in 2023.
The Reader's Guide originally appeared in the ebook edition of this work.

Library of Congress Cataloging-in-Publication Data
Names: James, Aurora, 1984–author.
Title: Wildflower / Aurora James.
Description: First edition. | New York: Crown, 2023
Identifiers: LCCN 2022057075 (print) | LCCN 2022057076 (ebook) |
ISBN 9780593239476 (paperback) | ISBN 9780593239469 (ebook)
Subjects: LCSH: James, Aurora, 1984– | Fashion designers—Canada—Biography. |
African American fashion designers—Biography. | Abused women—Biography.
Classification: LCC TT505.J356 A3 2023 (print) | LCC TT505.J356 (ebook) |
DDC 746.9/2092 [B]—dc23/eng/20230214
LC record available at https://lccn.loc.gov/2022057075

Printed in the United States of America on acid-free paper

crownpublishing.com

2 4 6 8 9 7 5 3 1

To my mum and my grandmother,
who taught me about the beautiful dichotomies
that can exist within women that can serve to
make us stronger versus acting as a divide.

Sometimes your only available transportation is a leap of faith.

—MARGARET SHEPARD

Contents

Wildflower

Prologue

Why did I decide to write this book?

I have always existed in a space of misconceptions—and while I've mostly not felt the need to explain myself, I've also come to understand the value of sharing my lived experience. Ultimately, the more we can understand one another, the better off we will be.

People think of me in a myriad of ways: The light-skinned woman with the nasally voice. The fashion girl from Canada. The founder of Brother Vellies, who won the CFDA/Vogue Fashion Fund. The designer who dressed AOC for the Met Gala in a gown that said "Tax the Rich." The entrepreneur who launched the Fifteen Percent Pledge.

All of these things are true—but there are so many more parts of me. Some of my story may surprise you. Some may make total sense. Other moments might be hard to understand. But ultimately, all of these fragments pieced together make me, and all of us, human.

When I first launched the Fifteen Percent Pledge, I had no idea that it would take off to the extent it has. I thought it would get a little traction and that people would think it was a good idea. I hoped that maybe one person would be inspired by the idea and try to do it. I never expected that it would grow so quickly—or have such an incredible impact on Black businesses.

There have been many moments when I've almost given up. Other times when I've considered closing Brother Vellies, especially in the early days of the Pledge. Being under-resourced is something I am used to, but then add the staggering bias—both unconscious and not—working against me and Black women like me, and the effect can be defeating.

But launching the Pledge had nothing to do with what was easy. And yet, I felt that I had no choice. I've seen how talent and capability are distributed equally—while access and opportunity are not. Opening the door for those who have been historically excluded is not just the right thing to do, it is the first step forward in creating a more beautiful world for all of us.

That's why I've always appreciated the idea that sometimes your best mode of transportation is a leap of faith. But it took me until this year to realize that for me, it was not my best mode; it was my only mode.

1

my mother's daughter

When I think of my father, even now, I mostly see his back, him walking away. And yet, I can still smell his cologne, an Egyptian musk, and remember the thick woven African textiles he often wore. His accent was both singsongy and clipped at once. He was tall and had black, tightly coiled hair, cut short. His skin was dark brown and smooth to the touch.

He and my mother split up before I was born, so I never lived with him, but he did come visit. And throughout my childhood, he called every evening to remind me to brush my teeth. During one visit, I remember him teaching me how to moonwalk in my living room, Michael Jackson's "Smooth Criminal" blasting over our stereo.

Beyond these memories, I have no proof of his existence. No photo or piece of paper or article of clothing. I am not even sure what he was studying at college when my parents first met. These are the sorts of details my mother preferred to keep to herself.

"Why are you curious about that?" she'd ask. "How will it help establish your sense of self or destiny?"

I do know they were together until they weren't. And that was when my mother discovered that she was pregnant. When he learned the news, he proposed getting married. She said, "No."

When I asked why, many years later, she said, "He had too many patriarchal inclinations."

To understand me, you must first understand my mother. She is brilliant and beautiful, with dark brown, thick, curly hair that glimmers the reddish hue of a manzanita tree in the sun. She has curious hazel eyes, a smattering of freckles, and stands five feet and five inches. Her weight often fluctuates within fifty pounds. I have rarely known her to shave her legs or armpits. She would consider doing so preposterous—unless one day, she did not. She is not a contrarian, but she does like to keep people guessing.

She was adopted as an infant and never knew anything about her biological parents. She once visited a woman who specialized in understanding people's ancestry based on their facial structures. This woman deduced that my mother was Inuit and Irish, mainly because her cheekbones are so high set. This means I may be a mix of Inuit and Irish too.

Her parents, Hellen and Wesley James, raised her in Mississauga, Canada, just outside of Toronto. They chose her and her brother, also adopted, to create their family, which is also my family. But I am not entirely sure if my mother chose me. It feels more like I just happened. There is a difference.

At sixteen, my mother protested the Vietnam War, sang in a band, and left home to hitchhike across the United States with her much older boyfriend, whom she called the Silver Fox. They were headed to the Woodstock music festival, and as she tells the story, they took acid on Tuesdays, LSD on Fridays, and missed the concert due to a broken-down car.

She left again at the age of seventeen, this time for London, where she took up residence in a Kensington squat and learned how to blow glass. She claims that she was the first female stained-glass blower in England, and while I have no idea how to fact-check that, or what it signifies, I do know that she made all the glass prisms that hung in our garden. I called them the rainbow makers, because they turned droplets of water into sparkling Technicolor bursts that danced around the array of things my mother grew, from roses and rhubarb to carrots and coreopsis—and sometimes psilocybin (magic mushrooms).

In London my mother also learned to make her famous chili. To be part of the squat meant everyone took turns adding one ingredient, often stolen, to the communal pot that stayed simmering on the stove all day. An onion, carrot, or bell pepper. A bag of beans. My mother's recipe has twenty-eight ingredients, one for each day in February, and is a dish that I make to this day.

My mother was in her mid-twenties and still living in London when her father died in a plane crash. He was an engineer for a Canadian royal commission that was creating a power-planning initiative for Ontario. He and eight others, including an indigenous chief, were flying in a Cessna on a research trip when their plane hit high-voltage wires while trying to land in bad weather. As a result, the Canadian government gave my grandmother a big chunk of money, which she subsequently used to take my mother on a trip around the world, to Morocco, India, and Japan, places that were all considered extremely exotic and foreign for Canadians in 1978. My mom and grandmother used this travel as an opportunity to get to know other cultures—and probably each other, as well.

Upon their return home, my mother decided to stay in Canada and go to university, which was where she met my father. She was going to call me Zoe, but then I entered the world still sound asleep, so she changed my name to Aurora, after Sleeping Beauty.

I spent my first six years in a tiny town called Guelph living with my mother and grandmother in a small, white bungalow. "Nanny" helped raise me. She had big, bright, clear blue eyes that were magnified by glasses, the size and shape of clear sand dollars, and wore silk blouses with big floral patterns tucked neatly into her slacks or skirt. She never left the house without her hair pressed and set, lipstick applied, and often wearing a fur coat. She even got me a mini fur that matched one of hers, which I wore over my taffeta dresses with Mary Janes and ankle socks to see *The Nutcracker,* our annual ritual. I thought I was chic before ever knowing what the word meant. "A man does not buy his wife fur to keep her warm, but to keep her pleasant," was something Nanny often said. She was a woman from a different era, old-fashioned, and always kept a linen hankie in her coat pocket with a Werther's butterscotch.

While Nanny defined "ladylike," my mother's style was textbook Bohemian. She preferred Indian earth-toned cotton skirts with drawstrings that ended in tiny brass bells and wore tube tops (without a bra). She almost always had fresh-cut flowers clipped in her hair and would leave a trail of sandalwood, frangipani, and spice wherever she went because Nag Champa was her go-to scent. Though every so often she'd add a spritz of a Dior perfume called Poison.

My mother worked as a landscape architect for Mississauga, the small city outside of Toronto where she had grown up. One of her jobs was to preserve and protect public trees. When my friend's father, a developer, cut down a tree that was on city property, she was livid.

"These trees are works of art that the earth has been cultivating for decades," she'd often say, adding, "Cutting them down is not only an incredibly violent act, but it reeks of colonialism!" My mother, having been told she was part Inuit, identified with the indigenous people in Canada. It was made known to me from a young age that Christopher Columbus was no hero, but instead a rapist and colonizer.

"This is not our land," she'd say. "We are guests who are obligated to care for it."

While my father's visits were fleeting, my nanny was my rock, and from her, I received unconditional love. But like so many things in life, it was complicated. She taught me how to cook pancakes, which we made together every Sunday morning before heading to church. We'd sing along to the *Mary Poppins* soundtrack, the volume turned way up, belting "Just a spoonful of sugar helps the medicine go down" at the top of our lungs. She also sang "Eenie, Meenie, Miney, Mo" to me at bedtime, in her soft, soothing voice while wiggling each of my toes, one of my sweeter childhood memories.

Until one morning, when I was sitting cross-legged on my kindergarten classroom carpet, singing this song to the doll I was playing with. When I got to the stanza "catch a nigger by the toe," I heard my teacher suck in air, as if she had been hit in the chest. She stopped mid-stride and turned toward me. Her face was pinkish red.

"Aurora!" she said in a stern voice that I had not heard before. "Come with me this instant!" She seemed upset and marched me to the principal's office. I had no idea what I had done. The next thing I remember is my mother arriving, looking flustered.

We never spoke about race in my family. All I knew was that my mom was white, my dad was Black, and I was somewhere in between—which at that point in my life, mostly meant that my hair was a little hard to manage. I was also the only brown girl in my kindergarten class.

I don't remember my mother explaining to me what the song meant, or why I got in trouble for singing it. But I do recall that when we got back home, she lectured my grandmother, who appeared confused and hurt. And now I understand why: As much as she loved me, she was a product of her environment. Racism is not a thing that can be simply named and cured. It must be actively identified and then consciously unlearned.

Nanny never sang that song to me again, which was hard for me. I loved the tenderness of those moments, just me and Nanny, her soft fingers pulling my toes and then itsy-bitsy spidering up my legs to my belly. While her singing that song to me in a sweet way did not make her any less racist, it also did not make me love her any less. Both things can be true.

My grandmother was born in 1916. She had antiquated views and they showed up in the songs she sang and the comments she made—she referred to all Asian people as "the Chinese." My father never lived with us, and I never made the connection between him and the way my nanny felt about Black men in general. She never said they were dangerous or to be feared, but I knew she felt this way because she would squeeze my hand and hurry me along or hold her purse a little closer to her chest if we passed a person of color on the street.

My grandmother also sponsored dozens of kids living in Africa, sending twenty- or even hundred-dollar bills in the letters that we wrote together to Rwanda and the Democratic Republic of the Congo. I did not yet have language for colonialism or white saviorism—I was six!—and still, these relationships with my grandmother's paid pen pals helped me understand the complexities of my privilege: I had food, education, and access. "Imagine being in Simon's shoes," she'd say.

"I know we are not supposed to send extra money, but just think of what his family might be able to do with this!" she'd say as we slipped more bills in with our letter. "Maybe they will invest in a goat and have milk for a year!"

It never occurred to me that I might in some way be connected to any of the kids with whom I was corresponding. I had no idea that there was a thread in my own DNA that would one day pull me back to Africa seeking answers to questions that were already beginning to take root in my young mind.

I was six years old when I saw my father for the last time.

I watched him walk out to his car through our living room window. Behind me, I heard my mother crying. She never cried, so this stands out.

"He's leaving," she said through her tears.

He had come to let my mother know that he was moving to L.A. with a woman he was planning to marry. She was pregnant with his daughter, my half sister.

Even though I never spent any time at his house, I still felt connected to my father through his visits. I did not know how much I cherished them until they stopped.

He did continue to call from California, to remind me to brush my teeth, but not as often as he used to. And he did send a Mickey Mouse T-shirt that read, SOMEONE IN CALIFORNIA LOVES ME—proof that he had not forgotten me.

2

Castles made of Sand

Several months after my father left, my mother, grandmother, and I went to Jamaica for vacation. We'd usually go over the Christmas holiday, to escape Canada's frigid cold, and the best part for me was the buffet dinner at our hotel in Montego Bay, mostly because it had a self-serve ice cream cart. One evening, toward the end of our vacation, I was holding a bowl of vanilla ice cream, deciding between raspberries or sprinkles, when I heard a gruff voice with a thick Jamaican accent:

"I can carry that for you."

It felt more like a command than an offer.

I peered up at a man who looked to be in his thirties and felt an immediate repulsion. His eyes appeared to have been dipped in tea, the whites stained a yellowish brown. I also noticed several earthworm-sized veins bulging from his neck.

Before I could say, "No, I'm fine," he snatched my bowl and said, "Let me take you back to your table. It is not safe to be alone."

That sickening feeling stayed with me as I followed him back to where my mother and grandmother were finishing their meal. It intensified as he began chatting with my mother, who seemed curious to know more about him, as well as flattered that he was interested in her. His name was Winston and he lived in Ochos Rios.

"I also have a place in Toronto," he said with a forced smile.

Winston was five feet six with lightbulb-white teeth and smooth Black skin. He was wearing jeans and Fila sneakers with a crisp button-down shirt. As he chatted with my mom, he put on dark-lensed Ray-Bans, which I found odd, as the sun had set. But I also preferred it because his eyes spooked me—they were dull. No flicker. Just cold.

"Oh," my mother was intrigued. "We live an hour away, in Guelph."

My mom was dating someone else at the time, but Winston had a lot of bravado. They continued to chat that evening and then on the phone when we returned to Canada. When he came up to Toronto the following month, he invited my mother to visit him there. Every so often, he would come to Guelph. I always knew when he was there because when I arrived home from school, I could smell the musky scent of marijuana seeping out around the edges of her bedroom door. My mom had always smoked pot, daily and openly, so that was not shocking.

But what she smoked with him was extra potent and thick, and, for the first time, behind a closed door. That struck me as odd, as did other small changes I began to see in her. She started shaving her armpits and her legs, and Versace belts replaced her Indian drawstrings. I would come home from school and instead of asking me about my day, she'd seem distracted. Or she would not even be home at all.

"Where's Mom?" I'd ask Nanny as we sat down to dinner.

"Oh, she went to see Winston in Toronto," she'd respond, smiling, but I could tell she was not happy about it either. Her voice was extra upbeat, like she was trying to convince herself and me that this was a good thing. I would slump in my chair, suddenly not hungry, while Nanny tried to get me talking. "What's wrong, sweetheart?" she'd ask, her blue eyes soft and searching behind her big round glasses.

I could not put into words the bad feeling I had about this man who was taking my mother away from me, so I stayed quiet.

When he was not around, my mom would take me on adventures to the science museum or to see a new art show at the Royal Ontario Museum. We watched *Star Trek* and ate ice cream on the couch and would spend weekends at my godmother Mary's house. Mary lived in a guest cottage on a magical and massive estate in a town called Erin, a thirty-minute drive from Guelph. She and her husband were the property's caretakers, which meant I spent my weekends wandering through a fairy-tale forest that was home to flying squirrels and hummingbirds that drank from the flowers Mary and my mother planted in the sprawling garden there. And this is where my mother also taught me how to make seed bombs: We'd put the seeds of wildflowers in a bowl with compost and clay and make small balls out of the material, and then on our drive home, we'd play this game. Whoever spotted an empty field would yell, "Seed bomb!" We'd roll down the window and throw the clay balls into those spaces and imagine the flower fields that would flourish there.

Those visits became less consistent as my mom's relationship with Winston progressed.

They had only been dating a few months, but I always knew it was him calling because she would smile, look off in the distance, and then leave whatever we were doing—eating dinner, watching a movie, playing a card game—to take the call in her bedroom. Nanny and I would hear the door click closed and the soft muffle of her voice. We'd lose her for at least an hour, sometimes more.

One day, the phone rang. And when my mother answered, I could feel the energy shift.

"That's just not possible," I heard her say in a voice more unsure than I was used to.

Whoever was on the other end of the line continued to speak until my mother slammed the phone back onto the receiver. Within seconds, it started ringing again, over and over, and it did not stop until my mother finally answered. I could tell from her tense, upright posture that it was the same person.

"What does this have to do with me?" she asked, agitated.

She pulled the receiver away from her ear and looked at it, confused, before swiftly hanging up, eyes widened, lips tight. She looked as if she had touched an electric fence. When the phone rang again, she removed it from the receiver, placed it on the counter, and walked out of the room.

The next day, I overheard her speaking with Nanny.

"She says she is Winston's girlfriend," her voice cracking. "She says she is the mother of his son Steven. They live in Toronto."

Nanny's voice was firm. "That is a sign: It's time to cut him loose."

I felt a wave of relief wash over me; now things could go back to the way they'd been.

A few weeks later, my mother picked me up from school. I was in first grade, and as I climbed into the front seat of her white Nissan 240SX, I could tell by her smile that she was in a good mood.

"I have exciting news," she said, beaming.

I began to fiddle with the cassette player in search of my favorite Cyndi Lauper song, "Girls Just Want to Have Fun," wondering what it could be, hoping it would involve going to get ice cream.

"I am getting married to Winston!" she said.

My finger froze on the fast-forward button.

"We are moving to Jamaica!"

I was flooded with that sick feeling I had gotten when I first heard Winston's voice. It was all so confusing. I felt like Alice falling through the rabbit hole.

"Is Nanny coming?" I asked.

My mother's fizziness drained, and her body stiffened as she looked at me, disappointed.

"No," she said. "This is *our* adventure."

I did not say it out loud, but I felt with every fiber in my body that I did not want to move to Jamaica. I certainly did not want to live with Winston. And I did not want to leave my grandmother. I was also confused. Didn't Winston have a wife? Or at least a kid? I was too young to understand why this felt rash and wrong. But deep down, I knew it was.

I remember many whispered conversations I heard as I watched my closed bedroom door rimmed with light that seeped in the edges, like a spooky halo. Both my godmother and my grandmother desperately tried to convince my mother that it was not a good idea to give up her job and home and country to live with someone she had only just met. But she was stubborn, and the more we begged her not to go, the more determined she became. The idea of falling in love and spending the rest of her life on a Caribbean island was too enticing not to try. Even at seven years old, I knew that this move was neither in my best interest, nor hers.

That June, six months after meeting him, my mother married Winston in a small ceremony at Mississauga's city hall, in a room with carpeted floors and low ceilings. The only flowers were the bouquets my mother and I held, and the white baby's breath woven throughout her hair.

Roughly fifteen people came, all from my mom's side of the family. None from Winston's as my mother had not met anyone from his family to invite. I had just seen a movie where the kid objected to her mother marrying a terrible person, so it gave me the idea that I could too. But I made a pact with my grandmother beforehand that I would not say a word when the justice asked, "If anyone disagrees with this union, speak now or forever hold your peace."

When the justice said those words, I looked at my nanny, who widened her eyes and discreetly shook her head back and forth at me. I bit my inner cheek and wondered what "forever hold your peace" would be like for me.

My mom wore a white linen skirt suit with mother-of-pearl buttons and had her hair done in four braided Bantu knots. I did a double take when I saw her: She looked unfamiliar. I could tell that she was uncomfortable, that doubt was creeping in. None of her friends were in favor of this marriage, either, but my mother remained resolute: She maintained that this was the best thing for her, and for me.

Several weeks later, in July, my mother quit her job, moved Nanny a thousand miles away, to a house in Fredericton to be close to her niece, and shipped all her own belongings to Ochos Rios, including her white Nissan 240SX, which Winston specifically asked her to bring. She kept referring to this moment as "our adventure" and painted a beautiful picture of what our life would be like.

"Honey, we are going to eat fresh mangoes every day!" she said with a thrilled smile. But nothing she could say or do would change the unsettled feeling I had clawing in my stomach.

.   .   .

My very first morning in Jamaica, I woke up to a rhythmic clap-thud-clap-thud sound. It echoed through Winston and my mom's new house, which was now my home, though it certainly did not feel that way. I got out of bed to investigate, and as I neared the top of the spiral staircase, I could hear a faint grunt between each beat.

I sat on the top stairs and saw Winston in the living room, wearing only his boxer shorts, doing push-ups. Between each upward thrust, he clapped his hands. Disturbed, I went back to bed.

Later that week, we were having dinner in the kitchen when a lizard dropped from the ceiling onto the floor by my foot. In one fell swoop, Winston grabbed a broom and thwacked the tiny, delicate creature, severing its body into two pieces. He then continued to chew his steak while I watched the two parts run in opposite directions, looking to become whole again. That was the first time I saw him kill something, and I will never forget how easily he did it.

Winston "worked in politics," but I never knew what that meant other than it felt like every person on the island knew him. We would drive through Ocho Rios or walk into a market and people would call out, "Biggie!" his nickname, which I found strange because he was quite short and slim. He always referred to my mom as his wife, and me as his daughter. We were frequently in spaces that were predominantly Black, and as a result, my mother was constantly referred to as "the white woman." It was the first time I saw my mother singled out in that way, and it was shocking and uncomfortable.

I spent most of that summer in my bedroom, which had a

little balcony overlooking the ocean. It sounds beautiful, but it was not. August is hurricane season in the Caribbean, so the air was thick and heavy. One afternoon, as I was playing on that veranda, I felt the sun dim. Over the horizon, I saw the bright blue sky turn a dark gray as the wind twirled metallic clouds into a funnel shape that danced on the water, speckling the surface with frothy whitecaps. As I saw the storm approach, I thought, "There is no way I can fight this." I went back into my room and hid under the covers while the weather howled and rattled the windows and blew the palm trees around, waiting for it to pass.

We had been in Jamaica for about a month when my mother and Winston started to argue almost daily. At first it was just raised voices, though sometimes he threatened her with a fist. It was still August, and the energy in the house was tense, foreboding.

I was in my room one afternoon, reading, and decided to get a glass of water. As I walked down the spiral staircase and through the living room toward the kitchen, I saw a woman named Joy whom I had met several times. She was introduced as Winston's friend, so I was surprised to see her completely naked and moving up and down on the couch. Her eyes were closed, and she was making guttural sounds.

As I got closer, I saw that Winston was beneath her, also naked. I had just turned seven, but I understood that they were having sex. As I walked past them, they did not acknowledge me, or stop. It felt as if I was watching a movie, like this could not possibly be happening. Stunned, I got my glass of water and went back upstairs to my mother, whom I found reading a book on her bed.

"Winston is having sex with Joy downstairs," I announced in a very matter-of-fact way. Witnessing this act confirmed the feeling I'd had about Winston since I first laid eyes on him. I knew he was bad—for my mother and for me. This was undeniable proof that there was a reason for the sick feeling I got whenever he was in the room.

My mother looked up, startled, and then jumped off her bed and ran downstairs. Moments later, I heard yelling and crashing. I went into my room, shut my door, and sat cross-legged on my bed, scared, unsure if this storm would pass. All my fears were coming true. I had always hated him and kept waiting for him to prove me wrong. Instead, his actions confirmed that I was correct, and that he was a monster. Even more terrifying was that he no longer felt the need to pretend otherwise. He had successfully wooed my mom to Jamaica. We were trapped.

The next day, my mother was covered in bruises. From there, the abuse intensified. He often used a belt, but our house was not the only place I saw a belt used as a weapon.

I had started first grade at a private school called Ioana, where I had to wear a uniform that consisted of a pink pleated skirt, a white shirt, brown shoes and socks. On my second day of school, I asked my classmate for help with a multiplication question I didn't understand. The girl looked horrified, and I was not sure why until I heard Miss Joyce call out my name.

"Aurora Hawkins," she yelled. Winston had registered me under his surname now that he had married my mother. I loathed it. "Come to the front of the class."

She sounded angry.

As I walked through the rows of desks, I could feel my classmates' eyes glued to my back.

When I reached her, she said in a thick Jamaican accent, "Put. Out. Your. Hands."

"Excuse me?" I responded.

"Put. Out. Your. Hands," she said again, this time even more forcefully.

I did, wondering what she might give me—a multiplication book? We had not yet studied our times tables in Canada, so this was all entirely new to me. Maybe she was mad I had asked my classmate and not her.

Miss Joyce proceeded to get a belt made of thick, worn leather from the top drawer in her tiny wooden desk. She was a large woman, almost six feet tall and heavyset, so I had to crane my neck up to watch as she lifted the belt above her head and then slammed it down onto my tiny hands with all her might.

That first slap stung so much that my eyes watered. The room stayed silent, other than the slaps of the belt and the sharp inhales I took between each strike. I refused to cry or look at any of my classmates. That was the first time I had ever been struck. It was also the moment I learned to hide my pain.

As I walked back to my desk, my hands stinging and my face flushed, I thought: "When my mom finds out, this woman will be in so much trouble!"

That afternoon, when I saw our car pulling into the school parking lot, I sprinted toward it. Winston was in the driver's seat, my mother next to him. I jumped into the back seat eager to share what had happened. I imagined my mother marching into the principal's office, demanding to speak with the teacher, making sure this would never happen again. Her eyes widened with alarm as I told her about the belt, but before she could utter a word, Winston interjected:

"What is your point?"

All the air drained out of the car. My mom stayed quiet, and I slumped against the seat, willing myself not to cry. I did not want him to see me defeated.

By then, we had moved into a big white stucco house surrounded by a security gate up on a hill at the end of a long windy road. As we made the thirty-minute drive back home, I looked out the window, swallowing my sadness. My mother stared straight ahead and did not say one word.

At that house, the backyard became my refuge. It was where I spent most of my time, wandering through a lush array of plants: I could identify each and every one of them, thanks to my mother, who taught me their botanical names and purposes. There were birds-of-paradise, hibiscus, and native orchids that grew off trunks, as well as fruit trees that offered instant snacks of mango, coconut, and guava. There was a small banana grove as well, and I loved picking the ripest ones to turn into banana bread, using a recipe my mom taught me.

I often hummed tunes out loud to try to drown out the thwack-thwack of the gardener, who spent most of the day cutting the grass, which was like the suburban lawns I grew up with in Canada, except that here he used a machete. He never once smiled or even acknowledged me. I did not mind. In the

garden, I created my own fantasy space, picking flowers or playing with the puppies that had been born earlier that fall. Winston had acquired twelve guard dogs that were half Rottweiler,
half Doberman. Two were allowed in the house, one of which
was the mother and she was pregnant again. I was excited for
the new puppies to arrive. More friends.

One afternoon, as I was trying to teach the outside dogs
how to sit, I noticed a young woman at the gate, waving at me.
She was holding a child. The gardener was nowhere in sight,
and I knew Winston was out, so I drummed up the courage to
investigate. One of the many rules of the house was that I was
not allowed to speak to anyone outside the premises without
Winston's permission. As I got closer, I could see that the child
on her hip looked to be about two years old. She could not have
been older than eighteen.

"Can you let me in?" she asked.

I shook my head and said, "I am not allowed."

"Can you give me money?"

"I don't have any," I replied, thinking it an odd question.

"Winston does," she said with anger. "Tell him that his son
is hungry."

She nodded at the child on her hip.

That afternoon, I told my mother, who was incredulous. She
confronted Winston that evening. He did not yell or threaten
to hit her. He looked at her, slightly bored, and said, "The girl
is lying." But over time, my mother would learn that Winston
had eight or nine children. With others, he said it was "just a
one-time thing, no big deal." But soon, he started to respond
to her with a belt or a balled fist. "Mind. Your. Own. Damn.

Business," he'd say through gritted teeth, a whack punctuating each word.

I began to see my mother's fiery independence dim. The flame that once burned so brightly within her was slowly being snuffed out. This was scarier than any of the beatings.

At school, I studied hard to avoid getting hit and to prove the teachers who made assumptions about me wrong. They put me back a grade the second week I was there, but then moved me up quickly and I went on to become school prefect. I made sure to do my homework and write legibly and that my white and pink uniform was always clean, pressed, and tucked in. Otherwise, I kept quiet. I did not mention Winston's rage to anyone. Or that I was scared of him and for my mother. It was my secret. Instead, I focused my energy on trying to be perfect.

One morning, that changed. Winston and my mother dropped me off at school as usual. I was walking into the building to await the start of class when a bunch of my friends came running toward me, eyes wild.

"Come quick!" one said. "Your father is dragging your mother down the road!" I was not allowed to identify Winston as my "stepfather."

Three girls surrounded me, and with a mix of horror and giddiness, each took turns explaining that Winston had pulled my mother out of the car by her long curly hair and was dragging her over the gravelly, potholed driveway that led up to our school. I clenched my eyes shut, trying to stop the tears. It was no use. The girls ran back out to join the now growing crowd of kids, parents, and teachers outside watching the spectacle. I stayed put because I did not have to see to know it was true.

I had a few places of refuge. The fruit trees. Watching a baby rabbit in the backyard. Playing with the dogs. Daily calls from my grandmother, whom I knew better than to worry with these stories. What could she do?

We did not have a landline in our home—even in 1991, that was considered a luxury, as the island had very little infrastructure. But my mom had brought a mobile phone down from Canada with a portable case she carried around like a purse. She kept it with her in the bedroom and would take it with us whenever we went places on the island. That was how we stayed connected to my grandmother, my godmother, and other friends back home. We also used it to speak to my father, who would call every so often from California. Hearing his soft, singsongy voice made me want to crawl through the phone into that comfort. His voice reminded me of moonwalking in our living room in Guelph. Of the spark in his eye when he laughed at my antics.

At the end of each call, he would always say, with a sweet laugh, "Don't forget to brush your teeth."

In my mind, he tried to call me every day, though I only remember talking to him a few times. In the beginning, my mom would answer the phone whenever it rang, but slowly Winston started intercepting calls. The day I noticed that he had started carrying the portable phone, my heart sank. I never heard from my dad again—but I did dream of him. Not at

night, while I was asleep, but during the day, awake, hoping
that he might come save us.

My nanny might have sensed something was not right, or maybe
she had already been planning the trip, but I was so happy to see
her when she arrived that first Christmas for a visit.

When she saw my mother, she gasped.

"Are you sick?" she asked. "What happened to you?"

In the six months since she had left Canada, my once-curvy
mother had lost forty pounds. I did not notice it because I saw
her every day, but my grandmother was shocked at how emaci-
ated my mother had become. One night at dinner, Nanny asked
my mother if she wanted a second helping.

"She has had enough," Winston said.

My grandmother countered, "I did not ask you." Winston
stared her down, the veins on his neck pulsing.

Another day, at the same table, my grandmother started asking Winston questions about the money she had given my
mother to buy property with him outside of Ocho Rios.

He did not respond.

My grandmother continued. "What are the plans? Who
owns the property?"

He grew more and more agitated, and then began to yell:
"Mind your own damn business!"

"This is my business!" she yelled back. "I gave my daughter
that money!"

He rose from the table. She did too. When he shoved her,
my mother and I both gasped. Those veins on his neck were

once again throbbing, his eyes squinted into two angry yellow slits. I had never hated him more than I did at that moment.

Another afternoon, I was in the back garden with my grandmother. It was difficult to enjoy her company because I was worried for her safety, but I also did not want her to leave. I was caught in that limbo of feelings when one of the house dogs escaped the yard. She had just had a litter of puppies a few days before my grandmother arrived. I called after her, but she was sprinting, frantic. My grandmother and I were getting ready to go look for her when we saw her in the distance running back toward the house. I felt a wave of relief.

As the dog grew closer, I noticed she had something in her mouth. My grandmother was with me and held the panting dog as I tried to wrestle the soft squishy object from her gentle grip. When she finally released it, I saw that it was one of her puppies, blackened and sooty and smelling like smoke. Winston had thrown it into a fire.

3

fool to cry

During the month Nanny spent with us in Jamaica, she and Winston got into many shouting matches. This scared me because it was not like her to raise her voice, ever. But what she did not realize was that, despite their fights, Winston was on his best behavior when she was there.

When my grandmother headed back to Canada, I felt relieved—for her. I was worried he might hurt her. But now that she was gone, my mother was back to defending herself against his violence and rage. The bruises were a constant, as were the tears. This stood out to me. Before she married Winston, I had only seen my mother cry once, on the day my dad left. But once we got to Jamaica, she seemed to be crying all the time.

The last thing I wanted to do was add to her sadness, so I stayed quiet. I did what I was told. And my hatred for Winston remained a secret that made me feel queasy whenever he was around. I have one hazy memory when he was sitting with me in the back seat of the car. It stands out as he usually drove, but on this day, my mother was at the wheel in the front seat with another woman. That was when he started touching me. I froze. I knew it was wrong, and that his preoccupation with me, a child, was horrific. And this experience pinpointed why I had been so afraid of him since I first locked eyes with him at that ice cream cart. I somehow knew it would lead to this.

I have other hazy memories of him leaving my bedroom. I don't remember the details of the abuse. I was eight years old, and it was too much for me to handle. I did not have the word for it then, but I now know this is a coping mechanism called disassociation. I did not tell my mother what he had done to me at that time because I already knew that she was battling for her life. Every time she asked him about another incident of his cheating on her, he would beat her. I thought if I told her, and she confronted him, he could very well kill her. So I kept quiet.

My only hope was Nanny. On every phone call, I could tell she was incredibly worried. After we hung up, I prayed that someone, somehow, would come save us. I read the Bible front to back three times that year.

One afternoon, I was lying on my bed, watching the ceiling fan whirring above me, going around and around. I noticed that despite the methodical movement, the air felt still. Nothing moved forward. I was stuck. That evening, I went into my mother's room and simply said, "I want to go back to Canada to live with Nanny."

My now skeletal mother looked at me, her hazel eyes dull but searching.

"She must be lonely," I said.

My mother shook her head, like she was trying to wake from a bad dream.

"You could come with me?" I suggested and saw my mother tremble.

Instead of answering, she burst into tears.

That night at dinner, my mother told Winston I wanted to leave.

"People in Canada don't care about Black people," he began shouting, enraged.

My mom started crying again.

"No one will think you are beautiful there," he continued. "Here, they will treat you like a princess."

We had been spending time with a family friend of his whose daughter was Miss Jamaica. Her mom's name was Norma, and she was the closest thing my mom had to a friend.

At this point, my mother was not allowed to eat without his permission, nor was she allowed to make or have any friends. When one of my mother's guy friends from college sent her a pewter bookmark for her birthday, Winston exploded. That beating was severe, and after that, she was no longer allowed to get the mail.

Winston allowed this relationship with Norma because he was so impressed by her daughter, and he had it in his head that I could follow in her footsteps. But I had no interest in becoming Miss Jamaica. I knew then that beauty was often the least interesting thing about someone—and could be a dangerous liability. I certainly did not want him, of all people, to think of me as beautiful.

This all confirmed my desire to leave. Winston continued his diatribe about all the reasons I should stay. My mom continued to weep. I knew then that if I wanted to be saved, I would need to press on by myself.

The next day, my mom called Nanny.

"Aurora wants to go home," she said, her voice wobbly.

As I was getting ready to go back to Canada, I asked my mother again, "Will you please come with me?"

"I have to stay," she said, more to herself than to me. "He is my husband."

Two weeks later, my mother drove me to the airport, where the flight attendant pinned a badge to my white cotton dress that read: UM. I asked what it meant.

"Unaccompanied minor," the woman said with a warm smile.

It was a relief to be back in Canada. Nanny and I fell right back into our old ways, watching *Mary Poppins* and *Full House,* eating ice cream on the couch, and making pancakes every Sunday morning. We attended church, me with velvet bows in my hair, ankle socks turned down twice to form a crown above my beloved Mary Janes. My grandmother wore her hair pressed and curled, silver but tinged pink beside her temples, making exclamation points at the end of the swift upward strokes of her saturated blush brush. We would pile into her car and belt out ballads by Willie Nelson or Dolly Parton.

"Such a smart cookie," she'd say to me. "Creative, just like your mom," she'd add with a wink. She painted a myriad of futures for me:

During a trip to Marineland, when I marveled at the dolphins, she said, "You could be a marine biologist!"

When we watched *Gone with the Wind,* snacking on popcorn, riveted, she said, "I bet you'd make an incredible actress."

And when I oohed and aahed at the way the sparkly pink enamel transformed my tiny hands as she painted my nails, she winked and whispered, "Aurora, have you heard of cosmetology?"

A doodle drawing of mine would wind up on our fridge: "Ladies and gentlemen, I think we are looking at a female Picasso!"

I was so happy to feel safe again in my grandmother's care. She also let me talk to my dad as often as I liked, which meant weekly touch-bases. It was so nice to speak with him freely, without thinking about Winston interrupting our conversations or lurking nearby. And yet, I was also worried about my mom. It was hard to get her on the phone, and when we did, she sounded weak and sad. I lasted four months before I asked to go back.

In Jamaica, not much had changed, including the dread I felt around Winston. My nanny was my lifeline, as were the now fleeting and far between calls from my father. On one call, two months after I was back, my father sounded so relieved.

"It is really good to hear your sweet voice," he singsonged in my ear. "I have been calling every day for the last few weeks, but Winston kept saying you were too busy to talk!"

"That's strange," I said. "Other than school, I've been here."

After we hung up, I asked Winston if my dad had tried to call me. Winston glared at me and shook his head no. I stomped off to my room, flung myself on my bed, and cried quietly into my pillow.

I had only been back a few months when he banged on my bedroom door.

"What is it?" I shot up in bed, feeling every muscle in my body tense.

He whipped open the door, causing the doorknob to slam against the wall. My shelves rattled.

"I didn't know if you would still be awake," he said in his thick Jamaican accent. "But I need you to know that your father has died."

He stared at me with a hint of satisfaction. I could feel him waiting for a reaction to cascade across my face. It did not.

"Okay," I said, feeling the anger well up inside of me. I knew Winston was cruel, but this was too much. He would do anything to keep me from talking to my dad. I was so disgusted by his lie that I never asked my mom any clarifying questions, though I do remember seeing her in the living room crying. But that wasn't unusual.

When I asked to leave this time, neither Winston nor my

mother fought me. The dynamics of their relationship were so entrenched by then—less violent, but only because he seemed to have beaten her spirit into submission.

Back with my grandmother, I was flipping through channels on our living room TV when I came across an after-school cable access special: A statistic flashed across the screen, stating that one in three girls would be sexually assaulted by the time they're eighteen.

Up until that moment, I thought I was the only person in the world to have experienced this. Once the shock wore off, a deep sadness set in. The program said that if this ever happened, you must tell an adult who will both believe you and help you find safety.

That evening, I told my grandmother what I had learned.

Her soft, sweet face became rigid. "Has Winston ever done anything bad to you?" she asked.

"Yes," I said, averting my eyes from her soft, crinkled face. But I could hear her breath change from normal to shallow and rapid and knew that if I looked up, I'd see tears streaming down her face. I felt terrible to be causing her any more pain.

But somehow, even then, I understood that this was not my fault. I did not blame my mom either. I saw it as his problem. I also knew that I was going to have to tell my mom at some point. And I was dreading that. She was still in Jamaica, and I worried about her. She spoke in a whisper whenever she called, as if she did not want anyone there to hear her.

My nanny and I lived for those calls. They felt like a lifeline, proof she was okay. We would sit in Nanny's room, her perched on the edge of her bed, me sitting cross-legged in the center, the phone in between us on speaker.

As soon as we heard my mother say, "Hello?" we'd smile at each other and then hang on her every word. During one of these calls, my mom said the thing we both had been wishing for:

"I am thinking of coming home."

"That sounds like an excellent idea," Nanny replied carefully, holding back her enthusiasm. I could see relief ripple through her body.

After she hung up, she smiled softly. "Let's hope we see her soon."

We did not know what had happened that made my mother want to leave, but I imagined it was something terrible. I also knew that if I told her what Winston had done, she might interrogate him. And then he might explode. I was still worried he might kill her, so I decided to wait for her to come home before telling her.

Over the next few weeks, she'd call and say, "I am going to try to come home next week." Nanny and I would get our hopes up, waiting. That week would come and pass, and nothing.

And then one day, my mother simply arrived at my grandmother's home with just the clothes she was wearing. She was so frail, a ghost of the woman she had been. Her once cherubic cheeks were sunken and hollow. Her bouncy curls were limp, lifeless. For someone who had spent the last few years in a tropical climate, her skin was oddly pale, which I surmised meant she was not allowed to go outside. I was almost scared to hug her. But I was so happy she was home.

We learned the whole story in pieces over the next few weeks. Winston had become so violent that one of the guard dogs became protective of my mom.

"He would growl whenever Winston came into the room," she said. Eventually a friend of Norma's helped her escape in the middle of the night.

"I brought the dog to the airport with me," she explained, trembling at the memory. "But they wouldn't let him on the plane."

She barely got the last word out before dissolving into tears.

It took a while for my mother to get back on her feet. She was nearly catatonic when she first came back, but after some time, I watched her slowly re-emerge. She began putting on weight; her hair regained its luster. When I heard her laugh out loud, while talking to Mary on the phone, I knew she was going to be okay. We were going to be okay.

Once again, it was the three of us, living in my grandmother's cottage in Fredericton. We played board games, went to museums, and spent time making plans for the future, in order to forget the past. In a lot of ways, this new chapter felt like waking up from a bad dream.

Four years had passed since my mom had met Winston. I hoped that chapter of her life and mine was finally over. And yet, the melancholy that followed me back from Jamaica sometimes felt amplified in my mother's presence. I understood at a very young age that she chose to be with a man who turned out to be a monster. That choice impacted her, and me, and everyone who loved both of us.

I had so many questions for her. One night, I asked if she was happy to be back home.

"Aurora, it is never exciting to crawl back anywhere with your tail between your legs," she replied. Her face turned stony as she spoke. I was only ten and yet I knew that it was never wrong to course correct if you recognized that you were on the wrong path. What she saw as a failure, I recognized as a win.

4
bruised fruit

Six months after she returned to Canada, my mom was offered her old job back working as a landscape architect for the city of Mississauga. She bought a house, presumably with my grandmother's money, and moved ahead of us so I could finish fifth grade in Fredericton. Nanny and I planned to join her in the summer so I could start sixth grade in my new school. Things felt stable for the first time in years.

Part of my mother's job was preserving and honoring the public green spaces in Mississauga. This was poignant because we needed to regrow our roots too.

Nanny and I spoke to my mom every night while she got settled. She seemed remorseful that she had put the whole family through so much stress and grateful for this new opportunity. When the school year ended, I was optimistic as we packed our bags to join her.

My heart raced as we pulled in the driveway of our new white three-bedroom bungalow with its hunter green shutters. There was an oak tree in the front yard and a small stone pathway, lined with well-manicured bushes, that led up to the front door. I jumped out of the car and ran ahead of Nanny.

As soon as my mother opened the door, the woody scent of marijuana greeted me. My mother looked sleepy, which was not unusual, but also not what I was anticipating on the day of our arrival. My heart sank. Something was off.

Then when she pulled me in for a hug, I saw Winston sitting on the couch in our living room, those dark-lensed Ray-Bans floating above his white Cheshire cat smile. A wave of nausea washed through my body. I wanted to run, but my feet felt as if they were stuck in concrete. Just then, my grandmother walked up behind me. She gasped and grabbed my hand.

Neither of us said a word as I followed Nanny into the house and over to our bedrooms. I was relieved that mine was adjacent to hers. My mom had done so much apologizing for putting me in that situation in Jamaica, and I was so proud of her for wrestling free. How could she do this to herself? To me?

Later that night, after Winston had left, Nanny exploded: "What the hell is he doing here?"

"He is my husband," my mother said, full of conviction.

I found this all so odd, coming from a woman adopted at birth who spent so much time explaining to me that we get to choose our family. Winston might be her legal spouse on paper, but he was the furthest thing in the world from a good husband or father. Nothing made sense.

Since my grandmother financed the house, she made it clear to my mother that Winston could not live with us. That meant he only came over in the evenings when my mother was home. I always knew he was there because I could smell the musky marijuana scent coming up through the vent in my bedroom, which was above my mother's room in the basement.

I never worried that Winston would touch me again—I was older, and stronger. I could fight him off. Plus, my grandmother was such a light sleeper that I knew I was safe, even when Winston was in the house. He never came upstairs once.

I still had not told my mother about the way in which he abused me and knew I had to now. It could not wait any longer. A couple of weeks before I started sixth grade, I drummed up the courage.

"Mom, can we talk?" I said one evening.

She followed me up to my room. I sat on the edge of my bed and said, "When we were in Jamaica, Winston touched me in a way that he was not supposed to." My heart was pounding so hard I could hear it in my ears. I looked down at my pink carpet beneath my dangling bare feet and could feel my mother's body tense up.

"I didn't want to tell you, but now I need you to understand why I don't want to be in the same house with him."

Gray hairs were poking through her mess of auburn and chocolate tendrils. Her lips began to quiver as her hazel eyes grew glossy with tears. We sat in silence for what felt like an eternity until she looked up from the ground and her eyes found mine.

"I noticed over the years that you had grown more and more hateful toward Winston," she said in a quiet voice. "But never in a million years did I ever think you would go so low as to make something like this up."

I was flooded with a sensation I now understand as anger. And that night, I learned that when women are not given what they need, they can't support other women. I learned that people are sometimes desperate to fill a void. And I learned that birthing a child doesn't make you a mother. I know now that I was asking her to realize her very worst fears and to reframe the past six years of her life. It took me many years to understand that her denial was easier than truly and fully accepting the realities of our situations. It does not make this moment any better, but it does make it human.

5
Lions and hunters

I began to rebel. I ignored my mother whenever she asked me to do something and put pepper in her marijuana stash. I would also talk back, sometimes yell. Every so often, she'd say, "You clearly got your Trini-temper from your father." My mom very rarely evoked my dad, so I clung to that fact: My dad, whom I knew so little about, was from Trinidad. And that connection made me feel a tinge of pride. I imagined him living in California with his new family, and even though I had no contact with him, my fantasies kept us connected.

Winston must have sensed the storm brewing between me and my mother. But he knew that he could not take advantage of me, so he stayed clear. One night, I carved a big line down the side of his beloved sports car with my house key. When my mother questioned me about it the next day, I said, "Hmm. He must have more enemies than just me!" He was now on my home turf, and I was emboldened by that.

And then, just as quickly as he had appeared, suddenly, Winston was gone. I never asked what happened, because frankly, I didn't care. I was simply relieved.

Several weeks after he left, I realized my mother had been in the shower for a long time. I went to check on her, to make sure she was okay.

"I am fine," she said from behind the shower curtain. "I just like the water running over me."

"Okay," I said, thinking that was a strange response.

"I had an abortion yesterday."

She was still in the shower when she told me that she'd found out she was pregnant with Winston's child.

"It felt important to not have his child," she said from behind the curtain. "Or to even let him know that I was pregnant."

Hearing the water rush down over her and pass through the drain, it was clear that she was cleansing herself of him. That was when I knew that she had finally let him go. At that moment, I sat down on the cold bathroom tile next to the shower and felt tears fall down my face. I cried for what I had gone through and what she had gone through too. The pursuit of being loved and learning how to love was going to be a lifelong journey for both of us.

But thankfully, that journey no longer included Winston. He never came to my house again, though I did spot him a few times. Once at the mall, and another time when I was walking home. I thought he was following me, and I told my mom.

"That's just crazy," was all she said.

Many months later, my mom did get a call. Someone had found Winston's wallet and her number was in it. When the simple black leather billfold was returned to her, she found a few battered credit cards inside, and then tucked behind them, in a hidden pouch, was a single photo. Of me, in my school uniform. For some reason, that was when she finally realized I was telling the truth.

"Maybe it was always about you," she said.

She was not directly apologizing, and even if she had, it would not have mattered to me. By then, it was too late.

By the end of sixth grade, I had shot up to five feet eight. I had read in a fashion magazine that weighing one hundred and eighteen pounds placed me on the underweight side of the BMI chart. It was 1998, grunge was king, and these same magazines called this ultra-thin trend "heroin chic." Kate Moss also famously said at the time, "Nothing tastes as good as skinny feels."

One hundred and eighteen pounds became my goal.

I kept a scale in the corner of my room, which had vibrant green walls, bright pink curtains, and a matching rug. I'd tacked up a poster of Dave Navarro, Anthony Kiedis, and Flea eating watermelon: In fact, the whole room looked like we were inside a watermelon. Next to my CD collection (heavy on Lisa Loeb and Janet Jackson), I hung a calendar where I would record my

weight daily. Maintaining that number meant skipping breakfast and usually lunch too. I'd eat one or two Chupa Chups lollipops throughout the day, and then at dinner, push my food
around my plate, sometimes slipping small pieces to our two
dogs, who sat expectantly by my feet.

My food intake was one of the few things I could control.
AOL Instant Messenger was popular back then and I had found
my way into several chat rooms, which was how I learned that
anorexia was proliferating across the country. I found comfort
in that: I knew on some level that I was not alone. I called mine
"Ana" and considered it a testament to my endurance. People
would comment on how "great" I looked, and all the while I
was on the brink of collapse. There was an internal tug-of-war
happening: I was proud of myself for being able to subsist on
less than one meal a day. But I also felt that melancholy gnaw-
ing at me, deeper than hunger. I was not sure if I wanted to be
thin, or to simply fade away.

Meanwhile, my mom gained back all the weight she had lost
and more and started dating a Sikh man named Liv who wore
tightly wrapped turbans and smelled of agarwood oil. For
someone who often said that she did not see color, this seemed
to prove otherwise—in my lifetime, my mother almost exclusively dated men of color. One night at the dinner table, as I was
actively not eating, Liv said, "I have this new diet that you could
try . . . it's called the seafood diet."

I looked at him, bewildered.

"You see food and you fucking eat it."

"Cool," I responded, rolling my eyes.

That night, I slashed his tires.

For all her infuriating ways and terrible taste in men, my mother often gave insightful advice. When I started running track in seventh grade, she said, "If you expect to run faster, please make sure you're running with people who are faster than you."

She added: "Also, long distance seems like a lot of work. Maybe you should do a relay? You can get much further in community, can't you? Besides, it's better to end up at the destination with friends. Wins are not wins if you are winning alone."

I started running with older girls and was holding my own. One day, my coach pulled me aside.

"If you want to take this seriously, you have something real here." His voice was giddy, almost gleeful. "With the right training, I have a hunch that you could one day compete at the Olympics!"

"So I would have to quit smoking?" I asked.

"You are in seventh grade," he said, as his excitement fell flat.

I shrugged.

He never mentioned the Olympics again.

I was in eighth grade and at Square One mall in Mississauga when a man, dressed head to toe in black, approached me.

"Have you ever considered modeling?" he asked.

"No," I said.

"You should," he said, and handed me his business card. "Come by our office and we'll chat."

I was intrigued: I had just finished reading Tyra Banks's book, *Tyra's Beauty Inside & Out*. Despite our sparring, my mom wanted me to be successful on my own terms. She would occasionally fill my bedroom with stacks of memoirs. Tyra Banks's was amongst Mary Karr's *The Liars' Club,* Douglas Coupland's *Generation X,* and Elizabeth Wurtzel's *Prozac Nation.* Tyra was the first Black model to be on the cover of *Sports Illustrated* and helped open the world of modeling to a wider variety of girls.

This was also peak supermodel moment—stars like Gisele, Esther Cañadas, and Naomi Campbell were gracing the covers of *Vogue, Elle, Harper's Bazaar,* and *Fashion* (a Canadian title), all magazines I subscribed to. I watched Jeanne Beker's *Fashion Television* with my mom and nanny religiously, and for all our differences, fashion was a great unifier in our house. Even if I was shopping exclusively at Goodwill at this point.

We watched seasonal collections unfold with the same fervor that basketball fans watched the NBA playoffs. My grandma was an Oscar de la Renta loyalist. "He has an adopted Black son, you know," she liked to point out. Whereas my mom was devoted to Stella McCartney. I loved Alexander McQueen.

While I knew that I did not want to be a beauty queen, I was intrigued by the idea of modeling for its proximity to the rest of the fashion industry. My mother took me to the agency, where I was signed that same day. I started doing jobs for Sears catalogs, local fashion shows, and even a campaign for a hairdye company called Schwarzkopf. I liked the money I was making. But I found it disturbing how often I was asked to wear an animal print, my Blackness somehow equated with an African safari. The people making these decisions were usually tall, beautiful, white, gay men. The most frequent comment I received that summer was that I needed to lose three to four inches off my hips, which measured thirty-seven inches. At that point 34-24-34 was considered ideal.

I was thirteen and already knew this was next to impossible for my body type. I was still subsisting on Chupa Chups lollipops and chicken breasts. Still, the people I met in the modeling world made it clear: The only way to be accepted by the fashion and advertising worlds as "aspirational," and therefore capable of selling products, was to make myself smaller than was naturally possible. To compound this, the designers I loved most, like Alexander McQueen and Azzedine Alaïa and Calvin Klein, made samples in a size two, so there was not much room for debate.

I was on set one day, doing a shoot with a girl named Daria, who would become a very famous model. We shared the same agency and it dawned on me, of the dozen models working that day, the agent was taking 15 percent from each of us. I did some quick math and realized that he was making more money than all of us—and wasn't even on set. That was much more interesting to me than being a disposable clothing hanger. I told my mom I was interested in becoming an agent and she suggested I ask the agency for an internship, which was how I spent the summer between ninth and tenth grades, working at Next Models in Toronto. My job was updating the models' portfolios by placing the strongest photos up front and retiring the less interesting work. I was also in charge of reviewing all the photos mailed by women and men looking for representation. I was to make two piles—"rejects" and those who "had potential." They thought I had a good eye.

As I built friendships with other models, I came to resent how often stylists and photographers would pressure women to show more skin than they felt comfortable doing even for unpaid test shots. I would see or hear about models being shot in sheer shirts, or topless, in situations that were much more adult than their ages. And certain photographers were known creepers and had reputations for getting extra touchy on set.

I began to see what I now know to be a fundamental disconnect within the modeling industry: Designers (most often male) sell their garments and generate wealth for themselves and their shareholders, while the model collects a day rate, and simply works for hire. I began to wonder, "Why do young women aspire to objectification?" Nothing about modeling felt aspirational to me. Rather, it struck me as a system designed to keep women down—and to reinforce that they are always replaceable, especially after age twenty-four. Even more alarming was that these same women were being weaponized in order to exploit other women and make them feel bad about their own bodies and selves. I realized at a very young age that this was one of the fashion industry's greatest sins.

"A grand plan constructed by the patriarchy," my mom often said as I grew up, and I started to see her point: Models were tools that reinforced the idea that women are only valued as sexual objects. At that time, nobody was interested in the models' thoughts or perspectives. But in small ways, I also saw how the work allowed some of the girls I knew to support their families.

"I'm going to quit next year," a friend from Senegal whispered to me on set one day.

"Do it!" I said. "Book Maybelline, and then buy out the block!"

Another disconnect I was feeling stemmed from how my mother taught me, from an early age, to understand fashion. She spoke about it as an expression of one's self and one's values. Clothing told very specific stories—about the wearer and the maker—and before I was born, she started collecting pieces from countries that she and Nanny visited: clogs from Denmark, cowboy boots from Texas, kimonos from Japan.

She would visit indigenous reservations in northern Ontario, often taking me along as a child. We went to the land of the Saugeen, Shawanaga, Cree, and Anishinaabe First Nations, and I learned how they would hunt animals to eat the meat and then meticulously save and tan the skin and hides to make into coats, boots, rugs, tarps, bags, and shelter.

On one trip, we saw women beading patterns and motifs onto mukluks, these beautiful soft leather boots. Each design told a story—some were obvious, and yet others not, and I particularly loved the secret codes and languages on the shoes. The women all sat in this room that smelled of leather and wood and damp earth. It struck me that they were all my mom's height, ranging between five two and five five, and chatting away with one another while simultaneously working with their hands, either sewing the bottom sole of the shoe onto the upper piece that hugged the foot, or attaching beads with a needle and thread, poking and pulling. I noticed the wrinkles around the corners of their eyes—almost all of them, young and old, had laugh lines—and they also had similar hands, both soft and hardened at once. I saw so many stories in those lines and laughs and beaded patterns.

I thought, "If we all have to work for a living, this is a nice way to do it. In community, being creative, as an extension of your own culture, which you then get to share with other people. What a nice way to spend your life."

Through my mother, I saw how clothing could piece together histories that had not been written down, but instead were made. I saw how stories were told through artifacts. We also discussed how disruptive and destructive colonialism was to this way of life. My mother infuriated me in so many ways, but opened my eyes in others. "Until the lion has their own historian, the hunter will always remain the hero" was a Nigerian proverb she shared with me.

I began to see the chasm between the fashion my mother revered, and the mall fashion shows and magazine photo shoots in which I was participating. "Who was the designer?" was her code for, "What is he trying to say? How is it relevant? Does he have a point of view? Does he understand the female experience? Is he trying to?"

She was more interested in the provenance of culturally significant clothes, and she taught me to ask, "What stories does a piece of clothing tell about the people who made and wore it?"

I did not realize then how her curiosity would propel me to everything that was to come.

6

passing

I was in tenth grade when my English teacher asked me to stay after class. She said, "I want you to know that your grade is three percent."

"Really? How is that possible?" I asked, genuinely bewildered.

"On some days, you get points for just showing up."

It was mid-semester, and I hadn't handed in anything.

"From now on, you have to get a perfect score on everything to be able to pass this class," she said.

That semester, I was assigned Nella Larsen's *Passing,* which is about a mixed race woman in the 1920s who presents as white. Reading the novel made me think more broadly about race and people's perceptions around different ethnicities. So often, as a kid growing up in Canada, people played this guessing game with me: "Are you Jewish and Moroccan?" Or, "Are you Kenyan and Southeast Asian?" Canadians have a much more global view of the world than Americans—so people often asked me, "What are you?" They want specifics in someone's heritage, race, and culture. "Tamil? Which Tamil?" They understood the nuances between each individual experience and would never boil it down to "Are you Black? Or white?"

I also started to notice that casting directors and photographers and even friends at school used words like "exotic" to describe me. Perhaps the most jarring experience, though, was when my friend Michael gave me the nickname "Aureo."

"What do you mean?" I asked, perplexed.

"You're black on the outside and white on the inside," he said.

He also called me "Squeak." When I asked him why, he said, "It's because your voice is so high, you sound like a baby!"

Many of my friends said that I did not "sound Black," which begged the question, "What does Black sound like to them?"

There were only ten Black kids in our school in total: I was one of three girls, and we were all biracial. Of the seven guys, most were recruited to play football and one was brought in on an academic scholarship. And yet I did not experience that comment as racism at the time. I did not even feel like Michael was taunting me, though I was confused by his desire to separate me from being Black. It felt like the white kids in my school equated Blackness with DMX and the barking woman in the movie *Coming to America*—and I was not like the Black people they saw on TV shows such as *Cops* or *Jerry Springer,* so instead of expanding their idea of what Blackness could be, they chose to separate me from it.

To complicate matters, the O. J. Simpson trial had concluded a few years before. Back then, every time we turned on the radio or TV, we learned more gory details about the white woman presumably murdered by her famous Black husband. The trial, as well as the public divide over it, greatly confused me. At the time, I had no context around Rodney King or any of the criminal activity happening within the LAPD. It took me moving to America to understand the centuries of systemic racism and police violence, not just in Los Angeles but across the country, that led to millions of Black Americans insisting that O.J. was not guilty. It was so incredibly confusing to me and it was not until years later that I truly understood how nuanced the Black experience is, and more specifically, the Black American experience.

When I think back now to all the media coverage and seeing hundreds of people holding FREE O.J. signs outside of the courthouse, I understand that they were crying out for the injustice that had been happening since the beginning of this country to Black people. O.J. was symbolic of that.

But back then, I was sixteen and the whole thing felt scary and hit too close to home with my mom and Winston. It reminded me of just how lucky my mom was to escape his abuse alive. Apparently, it reminded my friends, too, as every so often, when an O.J. clip aired, one of them would turn to me and ask, "Is your mom still with that Black guy?"

· · ·

My mother almost never discussed race with me—she made it a point to discuss culture. She believed that the way in which people see and understand the world and its events is uniquely tied to where they come from and how they are raised. Being "mixed," and the daughter of a mother who was adopted, felt like a great opportunity to be curious about different races and cultures. And to just continue existing as me, although it often felt like I'd never truly belong anywhere.

I did find it confusing how in TV programs and movies, Black people were often portrayed by mixed race people—and the villains were inevitably darker skinned. It felt problematic and untrue. I see now how I've experienced colorism my whole life, a concept my young mind was struggling to figure out.

I started thinking more about my own father. I still knew so little about him. What was he like? Who were his people? And so, who were mine?

I was seventeen when I decided to ask my mother more about him. She was sitting in her bedroom, rolling a joint. It was a sunny afternoon and the dream catcher in the window was casting a spiderweb-shaped shadow on the wooden floor.

"Where in Trinidad is my father from?" I asked, plopping down on the bed next to her.

"He was from Ghana," she said. "Why would you think he was from Trinidad?"

I was floored. She had always equated my bursts of anger to the "Trini-temper" I "inherited" from my father.

"I'm sorry, what? This is insane. So I am not Caribbean, I am Ghanaian?"

My mother took a slow pull from her joint and then stared

at the lit end intently before cooing, "Anyway, I don't see why it matters."

I felt my stomach do slow-motion flips. I'd never heard her mention Ghana before. I wondered if my mom believed that since she could not know her origins, why would I need to know mine? Whatever her reasons, from that moment, I knew that uncovering anything about my roots would be up to me.

"Can you connect us?" I asked her. "I have so many questions."

There was so much that I did not know about this man, who was half of me.

"Aurora," she said, shocked. "He's dead."

"What?" I responded. "Are you sure?"

"Yes, I'm positive," she replied, her hazel eyes narrowing in on mine. "He died of leukemia when you were eight years old. Don't you remember?"

I was stunned.

"You thought he was alive this whole time?" she asked.

"Yes," I finally said. "I thought Winston had lied."

That night I learned my father had come to Jamaica after he was diagnosed, and Winston refused to allow him to see me. I thought again and again about all those moments when I wished and hoped that my father would come save me in Jamaica, and the disappointment I felt when he never materialized. To learn that he had tried was devastating. I had spent so much time channeling these vivid hallucinations of what he had been doing all these years, fantasizing about who he had grown into. Suddenly, all those daydreams felt violently snatched away from me. The whiplash of Winston's emotional violence continued to accost me, even when he, too, was long gone from my life.

Looking back, I don't know if my not believing Winston was to be expected—since he lied about everything—or a coping mechanism. Regardless, I'd genuinely believed that my father was alive up until this point. And so, in that moment, I had to mourn the passing of my father.

"He wanted to share the news in person," my mom said. "But Winston would not allow him to come to the house."

I felt such a mix of emotions: All my conjuring as a child, longing for my father to save me, had worked. The thought of his being turned away was crushing, as if an anvil had been dropped on my heart. The sadness I felt was overwhelming. Not just for me, but for my dad, as well. I knew how cruel Winston was, but I could not imagine the pain my father must have felt in that moment he was turned away.

Thick clouds of marijuana smoke now filled the room, smothering the oxygen and making me feel claustrophobic. I was struggling to breathe between my sobs, tears cascaded down my face. I quickly got off her bed and left her room. I knew this was not her fault, but I could not be in the space with her. Why had this not been a bigger discussion? Why had I not been allowed the opportunity to go to his funeral? I knew he had another daughter—was she okay? It had been ten years at this point, so we had completely lost contact with her, the only other blood relative I knew I had in the world besides my mom.

Shortly after learning all of this, I was in a taxi in Toronto. The driver had dark skin and was wearing a pillbox hat in a brocaded fabric. His upbeat energy and lilting accent reminded me of my father. I asked where he was from.

"Ghana!" he said with a broad, capped-tooth smile that filled the rearview mirror.

My heart skipped a beat.

"My father was from Ghana too," I said. My smile grew as his eyes met mine, bright and sparkling.

"What is your father's name?" he asked, his jovial energy filling the cab, infectious.

"Kofi," I said.

"Born on a Friday!" he responded, with a grin so wide, his cheeks pushed his eyes to a squint.

I was confused. "What do you mean?"

He explained that often in Ghana your name is based on the day of the week you were born. That was the first piece of concrete information that I'd learned about my father's identity since discovering his origins.

Up until that moment, everything else had just been vague tidbits my mom had given me, a scattered puzzle—she said that he had a brother, but she had no idea where he lived. Honestly, other than that, I knew that he was a doctor. That he married another woman from Ghana, and they had a daughter. And that they moved to Los Angeles from Toronto when I was six years old. And that was pretty much it.

I began piecing these facts together and later asked my mom, "Is it possible that his family does not know that I exist?"

"That would be odd," she said.

It was not a no. It wasn't a yes. It was her reminder that very little is certain. That we live in a reality of unknowns. It was also her way of stopping the interrogation. Her way of saying, "I don't have the answers you seek." And that there can always be more heartbreak around the corner.

So I stopped asking her questions, since she clearly was not interested in sharing information. I knew intuitively that I should not push it—she did not know the answers to these questions about her own biological parents, so why should my experience be any different?

By then our relationship was defined by jabs back and forth. She might make quips about my grades declining and I would make remarks about her lack of a social life. During one fight, she told me I reminded her of Winston. In that moment, I felt my hatred of him shift to hatred for her, which then shifted to hatred for myself. I had this sinking feeling that I was becoming the product of an environment that I never wanted to be in.

At that moment, things took a dark turn. I started crying so hard that I could not even see my mother through my tears. All I felt was rage erupting inside of me, which turned into an actual clenched fist, which I used to hit my mother with the same intensity that Miss Joyce had belted my hand with all those years before.

As soon as my skin touched hers, time stopped, and my world went black. It was unnatural and irrevocable. We were both silent, and then my mother whimpered, and I wonder, in that moment, if by doing that, I had realized her greatest fear, which had become mine: that I had somehow become him.

It now makes me think of the truism "hurt people hurt people." And how cycles tend to be repeated generationally, learned and adopted at early ages. And how they often have to be con-

sciously unlearned. Whether we like it or not, we absorb everything around us. We learn as much from the people we hate as
from the people we love. I learned that unless I could actively
break the pattern that was presented to and put on me—not just
by my stepfather, but also by my mother and grandmother and
my own father—that I would likely repeat those patterns in my
own life. And oftentimes you hurt the ones you love the most.

In the same way that I learned violence from my stepfather,
it also makes me wonder who was the first person that hit him?
And how long are we going to let these patterns continue? It
points to a much bigger argument of blame: Is it the person? Or
the institution?

Winston was operating in a toxic male post-slavery reality.
He impregnated many Black women and then chose a white
wife. This fact by no means absolves him, but I realized, even
back then, how complicated it all is. And that we all have to do
the work. We have to actively unlearn.

7

Call me if you get lost

It was 2001 and the movie *The Fast and the Furious* was hugely popular, and so was street racing, at least in the suburbs of Toronto. I had several friends who were into it and I enjoyed watching the flock of brightly colored cars zip down empty roads. Meanwhile, I struggled to keep the 1992 monochrome gray Nissan Stanza beater that my grandma gave me from stalling at stop signs. I still would try to make it do donuts in abandoned parking lots and loved the rush of adrenaline from pushing that car to its limits, smelling the burnt rubber, and seeing the tracks it left behind. I was looking for ways to feel something back then.

The melancholy that first enveloped me in Jamaica was tightening its grip. It made it almost impossible for me to feel anything. Most days, I was numb. But I loved driving and being in control of my forward motion and soon was flooring the gas pedal to feel the adrenaline rush of being flung back into the driver's seat as the engine lurched ahead.

Kendall, my boyfriend at the time, happened to be selling his Mitsubishi Eclipse so he could get a new one. To keep me out of her hair, my mom gave me seven thousand dollars to buy Kendall's car, and with the help of my friend Rob, I immediately lowered it, painted it pink, added rims, and switched out the back lights for red-and-white Euro lights, as opposed to the standard American orange. I also altered the engine and exhaust systems so I could use NOS gas, which makes your car go faster, and cut the stick shift, to make it easier to switch gears. The finishing touch: He mounted a screen that I bought with money saved from my part-time mall job at Club Monaco into the dashboard so I could watch movies while sitting in the parking lot of my high school or anywhere at all.

My mom supported this new interest. Since I was young, she had always been insistent that I learn how cars function. "You can't just know how to drive and pass a test," she said. "You must learn how to truly operate a vehicle."

I started experimenting with street racing too. When my friends and I would stop at a red light, I would quickly burst ahead of them, and shift into second gear before they even realized what had hit them. In those fast, fleeting moments, both hands on the wheel, I was in control. In my Parasuco jeans, with a long, high ponytail, I was also constantly underestimated by unsuspecting men, written off to be the beauty and not the brain.

My car became my safe space. It allowed me to run away from my failing grades and my body image issues, as well as my mom's suggestion that I had inherited Winston's deviant qualities. It allowed me to believe that I could forge my own path.

My car was also my getaway: I'd sneak out of the house in the middle of the night, not to go party, but to drive an hour to Niagara Falls, where I liked to watch the water surge and feel the earth tremble as it absorbed that power. Every so often, a gigantic ice boulder would fly over the edge and free fall, before crashing in the frothy pools below and smashing into a million pieces. It made me realize that things that took a long time to grow can quickly shape-shift. A reminder that everything continues to move forward and evolve, whether you like it or not. And sometimes things fall apart.

I was in history class, September of my senior year, when I asked my teacher a question about the Native American experience. My mom always taught me to consider my sources: Where did the information come from? Is it accurate? According to whom? I challenged the teacher on the material he was presenting as fact, and his response was to kick me out of class. I was sitting in the hallway when I decided that I didn't want to be in high school anymore.

There were many reasons, from the creepy drama teacher who played a game called Drop the Keys whenever girls wore skirts to class to the fact that it seemed like everyone around me at my white upper-class high school was experimenting with cocaine and ecstasy. I never did those drugs because I did not like being out of control. Plus, my mom had tried them all, so *not* doing them was my form of rebellion.

I went to the principal's office that day to say I was dropping out. He was not surprised, but I knew my mom would be furious. I waited a full week before telling her.

"An education cannot be taken for granted," she said. "It's the only thing that no one can take away from you in life." My mom was patient and open to a lot of ways of being in the world, but she could not stand the idea of me being uneducated. She made it clear that while I might not have valued the opinion of the educators that were assigned to me, there was an undeniable value in attaining the diploma itself.

I spent a few months wandering aimlessly, unsure of what to do beyond working my part-time job at the mall. My mom was getting exasperated—if I wasn't going to attend traditional high school, she said, "you will do a correspondence course— I am not arguing with you about this."

Correspondence school, she explained, meant that I could do the bulk of the coursework at home, and it would provide me with transcripts that said I graduated.

I did not object. I was working at the Guess store at the Erin Mills Town Centre, spending my paycheck on low-waisted jeans that laced up the front, platform boots, and French manicured nails. I had no clue what I wanted to do with my life. It was a way to pass the time.

By then, my mom had started dating Thomas, the first white partner I had ever known her to have. He was generally dismissive and made me feel like an inconvenience. It was 2002 and he reminded me of George W. Bush—same stature, a little bit smaller, and with that same country, beer-drinking energy. I also noticed him stiffening up and getting quiet whenever he was seen in public with me and my mom. It was obvious that I was not his daughter, and that made him uncomfortable. I could never understand how a woman as seemingly strong and smart as my mom could spend so much of her life controlled by unkind men. I both looked up to her and, at the same time, wanted nothing to do with her.

That spring, my mom sat me down and said she and Thomas were moving.

I responded: "Again? You're really doing this again?"

She simply said, "I am selling the house; Nanny is moving back to the east coast into an old folks' home, and you need to figure out what you would like to do."

Despite everything, my grandmother had remained my best friend, the one constant in my life. Always there to listen and encourage me, and she'd even helped me propel my 3 percent to a passing grade when I was still in school. We had dinner together most evenings and I'd still accompany her to church every so often.

She'd come into the kitchen on Sunday morning in a pantsuit, her hair pressed and curled, smelling like lily of the valley talcum powder, wearing her fur coat, a Werther's butterscotch in her pocket. On the car ride over, she'd catch me up on the latest church gossip: How Ivy might not be there, because she might be recovering from a nose job. Or whose kitchen remodel was atrocious. In those moments, I knew how much this community, and living with me, meant to Nanny. But my mother was determined to move with Thomas, and my grandmother was never one to rock the boat.

My mom put the house up for sale soon after. I was so angry that one morning when she was hosting an open house for potential buyers, I barricaded myself in my bedroom. She started pounding on the door and I shouted, "I am not leaving." It got quiet, and I thought I had won. Thirty minutes later, the banging returned, even louder this time.

I heard a strange man's voice yell, "Open up!"

I froze, and then cracked open my bedroom door: It was the police.

They did not handcuff me, but they did take me back to the precinct in their car. My only experience with cops prior to that moment had been running away from them when they showed up at high school parties in the public parks. There was a rumor that in one of those incidents, they caught a senior and assaulted him. He was Black. But it was a rumor, and this was Canada. And for all intents and purposes we were taught that the cops were there to protect us. That was my feeling on the way to the precinct.

At the precinct, they put me in a holding cell for six hours, long enough that my mom could access my room and sell our home. I kept thinking of all the times she could have called the police on Winston. Instead, she called them on me, and when I was finally released, I walked the three miles home.

After she sold the house, my mother said that she was not going to continue to support me unless I went to college. There was no chance I could get into a four-year university, and she knew it. But I had finished my correspondence course, so I sent in a very late application to Humber College, a two-year program. And I got in.

My mom said, "This is how much your tuition is going to cost on top of your student loans, and this is your allocation for food." She also set aside an amount for car insurance, gas, books, and an extra hundred dollars a month for incidentals.

"That should be fine, no?" she asked.

In truth, I had no idea if it would be fine. The numbers seemed to add up based on my mom's calculations, but I knew nothing about budgeting or paying bills. The only thing I knew at that point in my life was that I liked going to the mall. Six hours, four J.Lo velour tracksuits, and a Tiffany bracelet later, car insurance was out of the question.

My mom moved to Halifax with Thomas and sent my grandmother to an old folks' home, making me feel like both my grandmother and I were still an inconvenience to her. That was the last time I lived with my mom, and it would be six months before we spoke in person again.

I had moved into a loft with my best friend, Ashley, and after I spent all the money my mother had given me, I finally called to confess.

"I'm obviously disappointed, but not surprised," she said. "You don't really have the forethought to budget or plan."

My mother wasn't going to give me any more money, and while my grandmother gave me some for food and rent, asking her for

it made me feel horrible. I needed another way to support myself.

"Don't get high on your own supply," is a basic tenet of drug
dealing, which made me a good candidate for the industry. I had
smoked marijuana heavily in my early teens, but I quit right before I dropped out of school because it made me paranoid.

My friend Manoly was a drug dealer in our Toronto neighborhood, and I told him that I had a thousand dollars to invest,
which I had earned at an ill-fated bartending job. He sold me a
big bag of weed and said, "Break it up and sell it in dime bags or
grams," which could go for ten bucks or so. Luckily, I still had
my food scale, a relic from my eating disorder days.

Every time I made money, I'd buy more weed and sell it.
The only issue was that my roommate loved pinching off my
supply, which cut into my profits substantially. So instead of
selling, I started delivering ten-pound bags for Manoly, who
thought I was above suspicion in my Juicy Couture cashmere
tracksuit. (I had upgraded from velour.) For those jobs, he paid
me fifteen hundred dollars. Bigger risk, bigger reward. I did not
tell my mother what I was doing. It's not that she would have
disapproved, but I think her lack of surprise might have broken
my heart.

My mother did tell me, "Find a major or you are cut off,"
since I still had not settled on what I wanted to do. I was lost and
searching, and advertising media sales was the only program at
Humber College that wasn't full. My friend Darren was taking
it, so I thought, "What do I have to lose?"

.   .   .

A few months later, I woke up to a text from Darren saying, "Where are you?" It was 8:48 A.M. and our final exam was at 9:00 A.M. at school, a thirty-minute drive away. I threw on clothes, jumped in my car, and sped to class. Just as I crossed the city line into Toronto, I saw the flashing lights in my rearview mirror and heard the familiar whine of the siren. This was not new—I got pulled over all the time. I was always driving fast, too fast. Usually in a race against one person, but sometimes three or four. Sometimes on busy highways, but more often at night on abandoned industrial streets.

When I thought of the most painful moments in my childhood—my dad walking away, living with Winston— I would press down on the pedal to stop my own tears. I was never afraid of dying. I was more afraid of the enduring pain of staying alive.

But this morning, I was just concerned about getting to school and taking my test. I did not care about selling advertising pages in magazines, but I certainly did not feel like flunking my exam. I had actually been working hard that semester, my grades were great, and I wanted to pass that class. I took my foot off the gas and noted that I was driving eighty-two miles per hour in a forty miles per hour zone.

A female cop's face appeared at my window, lips pursed. I braced myself. My experience with female cops was always worse than with male cops. It seemed as if they had something to prove.

"Honestly, whatever ticket you are going to give me, please do it quickly because I am late for my college exam," I said flippantly. She looked at me with a mix of irritation and spite, pulled out her radio, and without breaking eye contact said, "I'm going to need some backup."

I knew this was not going to be a painless experience.

She began to question me: "You have a TV in your car. Why?" "How low is your car? Why is it so low?" "Are these modified lights?" We were there for over two hours and by the end, I had two thousand dollars' worth of tickets. Worst of all, I had missed my exam.

Exasperated, I called my mom. For all my issues with her, and all her own struggles, she was brilliant at strategizing ways out of dilemmas like this one. After I explained the situation, she said, "Go to the courthouse and see if you can get the tickets reduced. This way, you also have court paperwork to give to your school to prove why you missed the exam."

I turned the car around to go back to the courthouse and was so angry that I started speeding again. The thrill of going fast usually made me feel better—so I shifted into fifth gear, desperate to be back in control. Within five minutes, I saw the same police car that had just pulled me over appear in my rear-view mirror again—lights swirling and screaming.

"Fuck it," I thought as I pushed on the pedal, luring the engine into third gear with the flick of my wrist. In that moment, not pulling over felt liberating. I wasn't just running from the cops, I was running from everything: Jamaica, Winston, my weight, my mom, the teachers who thought I would not amount to anything. I was slipping away into freedom, escaping from all the things that held a tight grip on me. But that feeling was short-lived.

Just as I pulled into my driveway, the cop came screeching in behind me. The same woman who had written all those tickets jumped out of the driver's seat with her pistol pulled and grabbed me just as I was walking up to my front door. She told me to put my hands behind my back and I did not resist.

My charges that day were dangerous driving and speeding. I was allowed one call, so I tried my roommate, Ashley. She didn't answer. But I was too angry and defeated to even care.

I was led to a small concrete room with a metal bench affixed to the wall and a stainless-steel toilet in plain view. I pulled the sleeves of my pilled, gray, woolen Club Monaco sweater down to cover my hands and took a seat.

I was alone for hours, watching people occasionally walk up and down the corridor, ignoring me. But then a familiar-looking Black officer walked by and did a double take.

"Why are *you* in here?" he asked.

He had pulled me over several times.

I said, "I was speeding and did not pull over."

"Oh," he said, amused. "Are you hungry?" I was, and grateful for this thoughtfulness. In some small way, I felt like he knew that for all my defiance, this cell was not the right place for me. He got me a small McDonald's fries.

The next morning, I was transferred to a jail in downtown Toronto. I had turned eighteen a few months earlier and was no longer a minor. I did not get to make another call, and no one explained anything to me.

I was placed in a cell with two women who seemed more comfortable there than I was. Claire looked forty-five but was likely in her thirties, with peroxide blond hair long past its prime. Her skin had open sores, and the smallness of her frame gave the appearance of someone who wanted to fade out of her own body. She had mischievous eyes that seemed to shield many sorrows. She was chatty and stood in stark contrast to my other cellmate, who was a large dark-skinned woman of very few words. Her clothing was oversized and baggy, hiding her shape entirely. She stared blankly at the wall for hours at a time, not uttering a sound.

I had no idea who was to my right or left in the other cells. I could hear people but could not see anything beyond the thick gray cinder-block wall. The first night there, a woman sang "Puff the Magic Dragon" all night in a high-pitched voice that sounded like a little girl's. The notes seemed to reverberate in the steel and concrete, slipping through the bars and bouncing off the walls. It was so eerie that I could not sleep.

Claire spent most of the time talking. Mainly to herself, but in theory to us, as well. After twenty-four hours of observing me cry quietly in the corner, she focused squarely on me and asked pointedly, "Why are you here?"

I had been sitting in the cell, lost in my own thoughts, wondering about my mother's accusation that I was like my stepfather. The thought was repulsive to me, and yet, here I was in jail. Was I becoming a criminal? How was this possible? I was running late for my school exam one morning and then imprisoned that same afternoon.

When I didn't respond, Claire asked again.

"Leave me alone, Claire," I thought.

By then, even my silent cellmate seemed curious.

"Why *are* you here?" she asked.

I had nothing to lose, so I told them the whole story.

"And then what?" Claire asked.

"And then what?" the quiet one pressed.

Both women were riveted and confused.

Claire asked, "Was there a warrant out for your arrest?"

"What is a warrant?" I asked.

The women on either side of our cell were listening too.

"Did anyone mention a lawyer to you?" someone shouted.

"No," I said. "They let me make a call, and my roommate did not pick up."

"So, you never spoke to no one?" Claire said.

I heard someone else down the corridor say, "This bitch is not supposed to be in here."

"Damn straight," another voice shouted.

Then, I heard a clanging sound, like someone hitting a metal cup against the prison bars. The tinny sounds bounced off the cement walls and down the long hallway. It was joined by clapping followed by more banging and stomping. Soon, all the women in the prison were using whatever they had to strike the bars, the walls, the toilets, and benches. They were shouting, "Excuse me! Officer! This girl is not supposed to be here! No one has come to talk to her!" The entire jail hall erupted into a chorus of protest, and they did not stop. I was crying again. This time, hopeful tears.

An officer finally arrived, annoyed, and asked what was going on. A woman from another cell quickly spoke up and began to retell my story, slowly and clearly, pointing out all the moments where my rights had been violated. She sounded wise and spoke with a determination that reminded me of a female James Earl Jones. As she continued, other women in the corridor backed her up as she underscored her points. I never got to see her face.

"We said, she ain't got no phone call," another woman emphasized.

"Uh-huh!" I heard echoing down the hall.

"Not right," someone shouted.

I was sobbing by then, trying to take this all in. These women did not know me, were not related to me, had never met or even seen me, and yet they were sticking up for me. They were becoming a nuisance to the system, which had violated my rights. They were expecting nothing in return except some semblance of justice. They were hedging their bets on me.

The cop said he would get someone to come talk to me.

Fifteen minutes later, my newly appointed guardian angel arrived. She was five feet two with olive skin, brown eyes, and dark brown hair pulled into a tight bun. She wore her mall suit well, with big hoop earrings and a silk flower in her hair. She wanted to know everything but also seemed too hurried to really listen to anything I was saying. I told her what had happened, and she punctured my story with questions: Did I see pedestrians? Did I run red lights? How much was I speeding over the limit? Did my speeding put anyone in danger?

Finally, she said, "I need a phone number."

"What?" I said, confused.

"Give me the number of someone who can come bail you out." She explained that this person needed to be over twenty-one years old, have fifteen thousand dollars in their bank account, and be able to make it to the jail by noon.

"I need to know their phone number right now," she said.

This was 2002, and I was flummoxed. I had a flip phone so memorizing numbers was not something I ever had to do. But then I did remember one guy named Andre, a former NBA player with whom I had gone on a few dates. Miraculously I remembered his number, but not his last name. She did not look amused by this but was relieved I had something to give her.

She said, "I am not going to have time to come back and tell you whether I get ahold of him or not. I am just going to see you in the courtroom."

I watched as she briskly walked down the hallway, her low block heels tapping in a hurried, rhythmic beat that made me feel a glimmer of hope.

The following day, an officer came into my cell with handcuffs. Once I entered the courtroom, the restraints were removed, and I sat in a chair behind a plastic partition. That was when I saw Andre. I got the sense from his body language and his refusal to look at me that I was not the first person to ask him to do this. Another person disappointed but not surprised. Still, I felt an overwhelming sense of relief.

I was released on my own recognizance, which meant Andre did not have to post bail. I called my mom as soon as I got home and told her what happened. She was upset for me and outraged at the system.

"Please don't tell Nanny," I said.

I did not need my grandmother to know I had been arrested. She was living in a retirement home in Fredericton, the town where she had grown up and had a community of friends and family that kept her company. But I knew the "Speeding Teen Model Gets Arrested" headline that ran in our local paper, the *Mississauga News,* would break her heart.

My mother hired a very intense defense lawyer. His first suggestion was that I go see a vocal coach.

"There is something about your voice," he said. "You sound high-pitched and ditsy. That might annoy the judge."

Ever since high school, people had commented on my voice. I was raised predominantly in Canada by a white mother and grandmother, so any of the stereotypical Black American southern dialects popularized on TV did not apply to me. And despite my time in Jamaica, any hints of patois had melted with the first Canadian snowfall. I saw a vocal coach for two sessions—he told me that I spoke through my nose.

I am not sure if my voice played a role in the judge's decision, which was community service and anger management classes. I do know how lucky I was to get out of jail. And to this day, I continue to speak the way I always have. The vocal coach sessions did not work.

My court-appointed job was to help unhoused women select outfits for job interviews through an organization called Dress for Success. I appreciated the concept: clothing as a means to imagine and facilitate new futures and possibilities. That was where I saw that the power of fashion, when harnessed correctly, could help women feel infinitely more confident, which could help them change their lives. This gave me so much hope. I finally found something I could focus my energy on—and maybe even a way to forge a future.

8

adrift

I had always loved dressing up and choosing outfits to reflect my moods—vintage sparkly striped Lurex Missoni that I found online for Fridays, or vintage Levi's and a faded Jimi Hendrix T-shirt on Tuesdays.

My mother introduced me to thrift shopping in high school, taking me and my friends to Courage My Love in the Kensington Market neighborhood of Toronto. She taught me how to scan a rack and spot the natural materials in a sea of polyester. Together, we searched for silk, wool, cashmere, cotton, as well as beads made from horn, onyx, bone, jade, wood, along with alpaca ponchos, shearling hats, and vintage combat boots to weather the snow. Now I started to think that the business side of fashion might be a career for me.

I was on MySpace, which was how I found Nasty Gal in its

nascent days: Sophia Amoruso sold her vintage finds on eBay and would go on to grow that online shop into a multimillion-dollar business. I was fascinated and flattered when she sent me a friend request. Although I figured out it was not because she wanted to be friends, but because she knew that having more friends would generate more traffic to her eBay shop. Her MySpace page was also a brand page for Nasty Gal. It was really, really smart.

That summer I had just turned twenty and was working as an agent at a talent agency to pay my bills. I had applied to Ryerson University for the fall to study fashion. One Friday morning, I had just settled into my desk chair when my mother called.

"I have news," she said, her voice cracking.

"Okay," I replied, wondering what could be so pressing at eight forty-five A.M.

"Nanny did not make it."

The phone slipped out of my hand and hit the floor. My grandmother had been scheduled to have a surgery so routine I cannot even remember what it was. Still, I had asked my boss if I could take a few days to fly to Fredericton to be with her. She said no, and when I called Nanny to say I could not come, she said, "Oh stop, don't be silly, darling, I will be out in no time."

"You had better be," I said.

"I love you so so much," she responded with a laugh.

These were the last words we had spoken to each other.

Now my mother was saying she was gone. The room started to spin. I felt hot and then suddenly, everything went black. When I opened my eyes, I was sprawled on the floor, my boss above me peering down. Another officemate appeared, looking concerned. Then I remembered what had caused me to faint.

Somehow, I mustered the energy to get up. I felt both frantic and claustrophobic at once. So I barged through the emergency exit and made my way down all twelve flights of stairs to the street. I continued to sprint down the busy avenue. I had no idea where I was going, only that I was trying to run away from the news—and a world without Nanny in it. I wanted to run to her, to prove my mother wrong. But then the tears that had been welling up inside me unleashed, a dam broken.

After I was able to contain myself, I called my mom from the street. I learned Nanny had died in surgery and that the procedure was riskier than she had let on.

"When is the funeral?" I asked.

"We'll do one in a month or so," she replied.

"Why not now?"

"I am leaving for Puerto Rico," she replied. "We'll do it when I return."

"Excuse me?" My sadness felt like a powder keg, ready to go off.

"Well, you know I've been planning this trip."

My grandmother had been the one who kept my mother and me connected, even in the moments when she was completely self-centered and thoughtless. With a sudden clarity of mind, I said, "No, I don't know. I don't want to know, and I don't ever want to talk to you again."

I hung up the phone and realized I was alone. My nanny had died. My father was dead. And I was an only child who'd just disowned her mother.

9

planting seeds...

I started at Ryerson that September, despite being told there was no space in the fashion program. I was on the wait list, and it was not moving. So, I chose journalism instead.

That semester, I saw *Wal-Mart: The High Cost of Low Price* in a documentary class and to this day, I am still responding to the impact it had on me. When the supply chain is structured around having the lowest prices possible, it is a vicious circle: The consumer wants things at a low price; the store is competing for the customer's attention by having the lowest price; and the factory is forced to lower the prices to keep the order, which means the factory worker bears the brunt as their wages are further reduced to make it work. There is a segment in the film that illustrates what that looks like in the factories in Bangladesh and China, where workers are paid as little as eighteen cents an hour.

All of this is fueled by the feeling, for consumers, that we are simply not enough, so we need to buy things to make us feel better. Billions of dollars are spent every year by major corporations to tell us we need something to make us feel more valued or desirable or successful.

After this, I became so enthralled with film as a form of storytelling, I applied to USC's film program. I was accepted, but I could not get a student loan because I was from Canada.

In a bind, I called my mom.

It had been four months since we had last spoken, since Nanny died. I told her that I had applied and had even visited the California campus. When I asked for financial help to go, her response was: "This sounds like a problem that has nothing to do with me."

The days began to seep into one another. With each step forward, I felt like I was taking another one back. I was stuck. Feeling lost and struggling with mood swings, I went to a doctor to see what I could do to address it. He suggested an SSRI. But I had just read a review of a book called *Skinny Bitch* in *Vogue*. The authors claimed veganism altered their mood and energy level. Intrigued, I went to Indigo, the Canadian bookstore chain, found a copy, and since I did not have a spare twelve dollars to buy it and take it home, read it there, cover to cover, cross-legged on the floor. The premise of the book is that you are what you eat, energetically, so it is better to eat plants raised by nutrient-rich soil and sunshine than an animal that was frightened in the last minutes of its life.

I was particularly struck by a passage I read that stated hamburger meat was not just one cow, but a medley of many different cows. That felt vile to me. I considered the contrast between modern commercial meat production and the original practice of eating animals that were raised and slaughtered in a humane way, in a community that used all their parts for clothing and shelter. The difference is vast. So I decided to become vegan. It helped with my moods and for the first time in my life, I was not anemic. I was getting all my iron from kale and spinach.

I ended up spending almost a decade of my life as a vegan, and while it was amazing in a lot of ways, it also provided a perfect ruse for me to skip meals or to eat in extreme moderation. So my disordered eating issues that had previously shown up as anorexia and bulimia transferred into the more socially acceptable title of veganism. While I certainly know many super-healthy vegans, I was not always one of them.

I started my second year at Ryerson and found a job working as a receptionist at the Yorkville Club, a fancy gym where celebrities like Robert Downey, Jr., and Jeanne Beker were clients. Jeanne was the host of the show *Fashion Television,* which had become my constant companion since Nanny's death. She loved fashion as much as I did.

Each episode showed a full seven-minute fashion show, from the likes of Karl Lagerfeld or Christian Dior or Anna Sui. Jeanne would go backstage afterward to interview the designer. These were not puff pieces: She had the vigor of a war correspondent. She viewed fashion in the same way my mother did—as an expression of one's values and point of view. She was always probing the historical and social context behind every design. I was in awe of her, on TV and in real life. And she took a liking to me behind the desk at the gym, where I'd often wear my favorite vintage finds.

"Issey Miyake so early in the morning?" Jeanne might say with a sly smile as I signed her in. I still shopped at Courage My Love, which was where I found that pleated Miyake look. I also had a giant black pussy-bow blouse, and a black leather fringed skirt from Exile Vintage, another favorite store. But my biggest score was a Dior Bar jacket. Jeanne always noticed.

Dressed head to toe in black spandex, with her signature blunt black bob and red lip, she asked me one day what I was doing outside of working as a gym receptionist.

"Studying journalism," I said. "In fact, I have applied for a job on *Fashion Television* a number of times, but so far, no luck! Perhaps one day soon!"

Her demeanor shifted from jovial to serious: "What was the position? Whom did you reach out to?"

She continued her inquisition before finally declaring: "You are far too chic to be working at the gym."

That same morning, at her suggestion, I emailed a member of her production team, Christopher Sherman, and a few days later, I was sitting at the *Fashion Television* office. Jeanne believed in me, and I credit her for giving me my first big break as an intern for the show.

My first task was transcribing every interview Jeanne had ever done with everyone from John Galliano and Alexander

McQueen to Tom Ford, which was like getting a fashion degree for free.

My mother was happy for me. We had started communicating again here and there. While working at the gym, I had developed a relationship with a neurolinguistic programmer who also did hypnotism. We had spent countless hours talking about my relationship with my mom, which led me to a few epiphanies not only about that relationship, but about the expectations we place on women who become mothers. Measuring them against the Clair Huxtables and other pristine archetypes that can only exist in TV land. But truthfully, my mom was like so many young women I knew who happened to get pregnant— that does not relieve you of your own traumatic experiences as a human. I wanted to give her the same grace that I gave my friends. And while I agree that it is critically important to be a good parent, in my own life I wanted to leave space for my mom to show up as herself. And not just as mom. Besides, holding on to my anger toward her was hurting me more than anyone else. It was time to let that go.

Within a few months, I was offered a job managing the show's website and social media, which included a MySpace page and a blog. It was 2006 and I was given free rein and decided to make my first blog post about how terrified I was to send that initial email to Christopher, an impossibly chic and tall and incredibly poised (albeit slightly short-tempered) gay man. When it was published, the office went quiet. Christopher walked up to my desk and asked me to lunch.

We have been friends ever since.

It was around that time that I started dating a Canadian rapper called K-OS. We met at a club, and he was thirty-five to my twenty-two, a hugely talented freethinker, with a soft spot for Molson Canadian, which he drank like water.

My friends in Toronto were vibrant, creative, and very social. It was hard to keep up with the pressures of a full-time job, school, and going out every night, whether to a bar, a show, or a club. So I went to a doctor with the intention of being diagnosed with ADD so that I could be prescribed Adderall—and it worked. The drug is also an appetite suppressant, so I got incredibly thin, to the point where I lost my period. I was going to bars every night where I'd drink so I could fall asleep, and then getting up again at seven A.M. and popping an Adderall to make it to the office by eight.

In the brief time we were together, K-OS and I fought often. Right around Christmas, I told my friends that we were through.

"We are going to L.A. for New Year's Eve, and you are coming," my friend Julie announced. "You need to have a one-night stand. That's how you're going to get over this man." That was not my style. I had only slept with two people in my whole life. But she kept pushing me so I played along. I told her I'd just done a story on "style icons of the internet," which was a curated list of people who were famous on MySpace. It included a graffiti artist who called himself Fresh. He lived in L.A.

"He sounds perfect!" Julie said, eager to select almost anyone. "Message him!"

I landed in L.A. on New Year's Eve ready for adventure. The warm desert air was a welcome relief from Toronto's bone-chilling cold, and the sky felt expansive, the city sprawling. We drove from the airport to a friend of a friend's house, where I immediately changed into a mustard-colored lace dress with leopard-print stockings, applied a messy glitter eye, and tousled my hair, which I crowned with a set of cat ears. Even I will admit this was a slightly odd look back in 2008.

DJ AM and Steve Aoki were headlining the party we were attending at a downtown L.A. warehouse that was packed and pulsating when we arrived. Blurs of neon American Apparel, acid-washed denim, shutter glasses, and glow sticks were weaving and bopping to Mstrkrft, Peaches, Justice, and A-Trak. I found a couch to perch on and was taking in all the hypnotic Technicolor chaos when I heard someone say, "Can I buy you a drink?"

I thought that was an odd question considering it was an open bar, and was about to say so, but when I looked up, I saw a gorgeous man, wearing a leather motorcycle jacket over a vintage T-shirt and worn jeans. I was struck by his cheekbones, two strong beams beneath sleepy eyes, and then realized— I knew him!

It was Fresh, the guy I'd interviewed. I had sent him a message through MySpace to tell him I was coming to L.A., but not that I was coming to this party. He was even more gorgeous in real life. We hit it off immediately, to the point that he came back to the house where we were staying and slept on the couch. From then on, we were inseparable.

My plan to stay in L.A. for a few days turned into two weeks. I quickly fell in love with Fresh. He was part of the L.A. graffiti and party kid scene, a smattering of beautiful, artistic, and slightly reckless young people, like Cory Kennedy, Katy Perry, and Mia Moretti, who were frequently covered in *Paper* and *Nylon*. Samantha Ronson DJed, and Mark "the Cobrasnake" Hunter photographed all of it.

Fresh had no interest in participating in capitalism, but made some money selling art and doing pickup work, like bartending or painting houses. With no real job, he could come back to Toronto with me. But he didn't have any government-issued ID, so he was turned away the first time he tried to enter Canada, and then held at customs for six hours the second time before finally getting through.

The first several weeks we spent together, I showed him around. When Fresh saw an ad in Kensington Market for a break-dancing contest that had a cash prize, he entered, and very easily won. He marveled at the fact that we had a cannabis café three blocks from our house—pointing out that it would never happen in California. He was even considering moving to Canada, until I woke up feeling nauseous. My boobs were swollen and later that afternoon, a doctor confirmed I was pregnant. My mother had raised me to believe that bringing a life into this world should happen when the time feels right—and not when you happened to have sex. She had been talking to me about reproductive rights long before I was capable of conceiving. She also knew Dr. Henry Morgentaler, who went to jail for performing abortions on women when it was still illegal in Canada. Being pro-choice and having autonomy over your own body were central beliefs in our house.

But Fresh was conflicted. I did not know much about his background other than his mom, who was Filipina, met his dad, who was Black, on *Soul Train,* and his mom raised him on her own. I agreed to sit with it for a few days, to give him time to process the news.

One afternoon, I went to the grocery store and when I returned, Fresh wasn't at the apartment. Something felt strange so I began calling his phone. It had been switched off. I was trying to process the idea that he might have just left me when I remembered that he had saved his mom's number on my phone. I called her and learned that he was on a Greyhound bus heading back to L.A. Before she hung up on me, she said, "How do we even know that it's his kid?" I put down the phone and burst into tears.

Getting an abortion was an easy choice. I never saw myself having a child in my twenties, and certainly not with a person who had left my life almost as abruptly as he had entered it. I started trying to move on, and when a couple of my friends invited me to spend my birthday in L.A. that summer, I figured it was time to go create some new memories there.

One night, I had too many drinks and called Fresh. He answered. He was apologetic, and kind, and my bar for male behavior was low enough that I felt okay to let his behavior slide. We picked up where we'd left off and I decided to stay in L.A. Back in Toronto, my roommates sold my belongings to cover my share of the rent: all my Missoni and Issey Miyake thrift and eBay finds, and that Dior Bar jacket. Thankfully, they held on to my grandmother's fur.

I had never considered moving to America—but Barack Obama was on the campaign trail and hearing him speak sparked something in my heart. I had limited understanding of the insidious racial issues in America, and everything seemed like it would be okay every time I saw him onstage. After the George Bush presidency, it felt like the United States was at a turning point and I was into it.

Things were complicated between Fresh's mother and me. Ever since our phone conversation in Canada, I was cautious, and the more time I spent with her, the more careful I became. She ran a series of convalescent homes, where the government paid her to house the homeless and disabled. I discovered that in many ways, it was not good. There was the assumption that she was going to take care of these people, which included providing them three nutritious meals a day and a healthy environment. The reality could not have been further from the truth.

Fresh had grown up in a small room in a six-bedroom house in South L.A. that his mom converted into single room occupancy housing. That was where we lived for our first six months together. During that time, I witnessed what I saw as a profoundly American way of providing care for these individuals: None of his mother's "clients" had access to the medical resources or psychiatric support they needed. She was being paid to house and feed them, and yet there were padlocks on the refrigerator in the shared kitchen. Some people were so handicapped, they could not feed themselves.

One client was a young guy who was a double amputee. He had developmental issues and had done some acting work in military videos. He used that income to buy movie memorabilia and otherwise subsisted on Doritos and Twinkies. I wondered if this could ever happen in Canada, where healthcare is universal and people with medical needs can get support from the government.

I felt an urgent need to find our own place. The problem was that I did not have a work visa or green card, which meant I could not get a legal job, so Fresh started working at a frozen yogurt shop called Pinkberry. And I began frequenting Salvation Army shops and other thrift stores on the hunt for valuable finds, spotting Dior, Yves Saint Laurent, and one time even a Chanel tweed, which I would sell to high-end consignment stores on Melrose.

One day, while thrifting, I came across an entire rack of 7 for All Mankind jeans, which were very in demand back then. When I asked the salesclerk where they had come from, she explained, "We get the runovers and rejects from the L.A. garment district. The items with the weird seams, off colors, or odd sizes."

I had all kinds of questions, and she was extremely knowledgeable. She explained that all the clothes that don't sell at the Goodwill and Salvation Army shops across the country are shipped to various parts of Africa. It is a three-part journey: The clothes we clear out of closets and give to Goodwill that don't get resold to other Americans are then shipped off to Africa. It made me think of how every year, my grandmother and I would do a "spring cleaning" and place all of the clothes we no longer wanted into a bag, which we donated to our local Goodwill. I imagined my stained Disney princess T-shirt or too-small and slightly scuffed sneakers making it to someone in my former pen pal Simon's family.

"How strange," I said, all these thoughts swirling in my head.

"One man's trash is another man's treasure," she said with a smile.

Fascinated by this concept, I started to do some research and learned how disingenuous and destructive that charity ruse is, as these clothes almost never, as we are led to believe, wind up in the hands of families in need.

This charity narrative is simply intended to make American consumers feel better about their consumption levels. Americans think of themselves as generous for giving clothes to people in African countries, whereas in reality, the process is a Trojan horse of cheaply made, non-biodegradable clothing that is often not donated to people in need, but instead either sold at local markets or, worse, sent straight to a landfill.

For example, the NFL makes shirts for both teams that play in the Super Bowl every year, but only the winning team's product goes to market. The retail price for one covers the production of both—and the losing team's shirts are sent to Kenya or Uganda or another country under the guise of a donation. It's a double incentive for the clothing company, which gets a tax write-off and does not have to deal with the waste.

Learning more about this process helped me understand Fresh's aversion to American capitalism; there was nothing generous or good about what these companies did. And since he had no interest whatsoever in participating in any system, I was determined to start making a living wage so we could move out of his mother's housing scheme and into our own apartment.

We had decided to get married on a whim. We were in love, and I wanted to stay in Los Angeles, so we had a small ceremony at city hall and became known in our friend group as the married couple, which was sweet. It was around then that Kelly Cutrone reached out to me, via Facebook. She starred in *The Hills,* a wildly popular reality TV show that followed the lives of three women who interned at *Teen Vogue* and her PR firm, People's Revolution. Kelly had heard that I was a determined and colorful fashion girl from Toronto and suggested that I come by for an interview.

I decided I had nothing to lose, so I went to her office, where Kelly and the producer peppered me with questions like: How did I support myself? To whom was I married? What did he do? Did I see myself staying in that relationship? Did we like to go out at night? Did I see myself getting along with the other girls? It felt like a bizarre line of questioning for what I thought was an entry-level PR job.

That same afternoon, they took me downstairs to the set where they were filming Lauren Conrad and Stephanie Pratt, and Kelly introduced me.

"This is Aurora," she announced. "She just moved here from Toronto and has an *actual* background in fashion." I realized then that the camera was rolling. I had not been officially offered a job, nor had I signed any contract, and yet, there I was, potentially in an episode of this show. I froze and stared blankly at the other girls, then made awkward small talk, before I turned around and walked out. That was not what I wanted.

I continued my search for an actual career and saw a Fashionista.com ad: Charlotte Harper, a designer, whose name

I have changed, owned a fashion accessory company called Harper Wolf, was looking for an assistant. I applied and got the job.

Charlotte was British, had a penchant for crass swearing and a dedication to skipping meals. She had been childhood friends with Alexander McQueen, but her own design aesthetic was decidedly L.A.: She was known for a scarf with a skull pattern, which she had copied from her production manager's forearm tattoo. She also made handbags worn by Halle Berry, Lindsay Lohan, and Nicole Richie, the "it girls" of the moment.

One of my tasks was to work with public relations firms in L.A. and N.Y. to get celebrities photographed with Harper Wolf bags. I would then flip those images to press agencies in Asia that would place them in tabloids, because getting a placement on Paris Hilton, Britney Spears, or Lindsay Lohan translated to lucrative sales there.

In addition to tracking who wore what where, my job was to do whatever ridiculous thing Charlotte wanted, like drive to Palm Springs to pick up two French bulldogs, one for her and the other for Heidi Klum, who, I learned after picking up both, did not actually want the puppy. Now my job included taking care of both dogs, which Charlotte named Haley Harper and Willy Wolf, and entailed driving to Malibu on Saturday mornings to sit in the car with them while Charlotte had brunch.

I had been working for Charlotte for six months when she told me that I was the best assistant she had ever had, so I was surprised when she fired me two months later. I asked her COO what happened.

"Someone new applied," she explained. "Her résumé was

amazing, and you opened her eyes to what a good assistant can look like. She thought, 'Hey, why not try to find someone even better?'"

I was upset. But it did not surprise me. For all I know, she might have thought I did not properly represent her brand. *The Devil Wears Prada* had premiered the year before and Anne Hathaway's character had it comparatively easy: Charlotte would throw things, scream profanities, and at times walk around the office completely naked. For a nine-dollar-an-hour job, it was just not worth it.

I applied for a job at Gen Art, which was started by a bunch of college grads in the mid-nineties as an accelerator for emerging fashion designers, visual artists, and filmmakers. The concept was to support creative people through events that promoted and shared their work with potential clients and collectors. By the time I started working for them in 2008, the organization had offices in Los Angeles, New York, San Francisco, Miami, and Chicago and was orchestrating sponsorship collaborations between designers and major corporations. So many amazing fashion brands got early support from Gen Art, including Phillip Lim, Derek Lam, Zac Posen, Rick Owens, and Rodarte. I started as an intern but quickly got hired to help run events—at fashion week and beyond—and to work with the curatorial team choosing designers and then building sponsorship programs for them.

I loved my new job: Instead of hunting for designer labels in thrift stores to resell, I was now looking for young talent to support. That was how I found Ace and Jig, a pair of textile-obsessed best friends; Hillary Taymour, operating under the brand name Collina Strada, which crafted quirky but functional leather bags; and Chris Stamp, a friend of Fresh's, with a streetwear brand based in West Hollywood.

Working with these designers, I started to see the difference between talent and resources. People would send me look books: If they had money, they could hire a professional photographer and models, as well as sample makers and graphic designers. Or, for six figures, they could hire the Launch Collective, an agency that helps start companies. It was through the Launch Collective that Liya Kebede started lemlem, and Pamela Love grew her namesake jewelry label.

Even if you had the resources to launch, you still had to come up with the money to participate in fashion shows, which had turned into such major spectacles that most designers couldn't afford to do them. To offset costs, brand partners had become a necessary accoutrement in the fashion world.

While my Canadian friends were receiving stipends and grants from the government, creating public art installations and vibrant music videos, I saw a dire need for creative people in America to be supported. Gen Art found ways to do this through corporate money. But there were trade-offs, and I will never forget the year Botox was a sponsor for L.A. Fashion Week. I understood the need, but in many cases the money that was available was not the money a designer would want to align with.

Eventually, I saw how often success had little to do with talent. It was especially hard to see designers put all their efforts into these fashion shows hoping that Barneys or Nordstrom would buy their collection only to be disappointed when the retail giants chose a safer bet. I started to think of it like college: Being an entrepreneur is the major—understanding production, quality control, pricing, customer service, the list goes on. Meanwhile, the actual passion, the clothes, is the minor.

I also started to see all the ways mass consumption and profitability were usurping the art in fashion. Jeanne Beker and Hamish Bowles and André Leon Talley and Tim Blanks were rare birds in the industry. They were fashion historians who understood fashion as an art form, not just a means of consumption and shareholder value. Most of the fashion editors were simply looking at what Nicole Richie wore as she strolled out of LAX. It made me wonder, "Is this fashion as art form? Or clothing as a consumption form? What are we really doing here?"

I was overwhelmed by the pace of the industry. I was encountering a system that felt hell-bent on selling product at all costs while promoting ageism and racism and body dysmorphia. The models were too young, and the expectations of their body weight triggered me. I knew how impossible and unhealthy that was for many, if not all, girls, myself included. And at the time, campaign photos by Terry Richardson covered the streets of New York, depicting women in what seemed to me to be slightly abusive situations.

On top of that, people in fashion did not seem happy. Even after a seven-minute show that went beautifully, there was a glumness. I was realizing this was not anything I wanted to be part of, and I wanted to focus on something that felt more real and joyful.

When Fresh and I finally moved into a small cottage in Los Feliz with a tiny garden in the front yard, I understood how much I missed nature in my life. The very first thing I did was fill our home, inside and out, with plants. I felt immediately better, more hopeful, less alone. The more time I spent in my own garden, the more I understood nature was missing from my life.

One afternoon, while hanging out with Fresh, I had an epiphany. We had lived in an eight-by-ten living room for our first months in L.A. and it was grim. And yet, I knew that so many people lived that way, and so I thought, "What if we could hang plants on walls? And turn these small spaces into tiny oases?" The more I considered it, the more excited I got. For me, taking care of a living, beautiful plant can curb loneliness. The relationship is symbiotic—you give it water and sunlight, and you both grow. When you exhale, it inhales, and one day it may even bear fruit, or the wildest, most beautiful flower.

This was my path, I decided. I just needed to figure out how to do it. I called my mother, who was still living with Thomas in Halifax.

"Mom, I want to put plants on the walls in rooms," I said. "I think it would make me a lot happier. Is it even possible?"

"Well, you would need a vertical planting mechanism that would allow the soil to be contained, but would also allow for the plant to breathe," she explained. "And then access to sunlight and water. But sure, it's possible."

That was all I needed. I called my boss at Gen Art and said, by way of a resignation, "I don't want to do this whole fashion thing anymore. I want to figure out how to get plants on the walls."

He laughed and said, "That is totally insane, except I just had lunch with a friend who started a business doing precisely that."

10
Seeking Sunlight

Miguel Nelson had just started a company called Woolly Pocket that created planting containers out of a felt-like fabric made from recycled plastic water bottles, which was shaped into pockets that could be attached to walls with screws: This was my fantasy realized.

Excited, I called him that same day, and he told me emphatically, "The world needs more plants!" His company's mission was to make installing gardens in urban landscapes easy. He also wanted to make gardening cool. I felt as if I had found a kindred spirit. By the end of our call, he offered me a job, as one of his first employees. There was no conversation about a 401(k) or health insurance or a salary—I did not even think to ask. I was simply thrilled to do this work that so deeply aligned with how I was feeling at that moment in my life.

The next day, I reported for work to a converted auto show-room in the Koreatown section of downtown L.A. It was a large, airy, open space that doubled as Miguel's home, with a wall displaying pockets filled with ferns and orchids and brome-liads. The rich and loamy scent of fresh soil mixed with the sweetness of Le Labo Santal 26 candles, which were lit through-out the space. Vintage glass lanterns in amber and jade hung above a huge, mustard-colored velvet sofa, and a movie-theater-sized screen played a loop of the 1970 Rolling Stones documen-tary, *Gimme Shelter,* alternating with the 1978 film *The Secret Life of Plants*. The garage doors, which remained open on L.A.'s perpetually sunny days, meant hummingbirds darting around the jasmine and wisteria planted outside and sometimes flutter-ing in to investigate the vertical gardens. It was an urban version of my godmother's garden.

I did not know that I would be getting an MBA in how to grow a business. At that point, Miguel had sold just thirty thou-sand dollars in pockets. But three days after our initial phone call, I was flying to New York to install a living wall on Martha Stewart's TV show. Together, Martha, Miguel, and I trans-formed a sterile space into a lush vertical garden, full of philo-dendrons mixed with ferns, pothos, and bromeliads.

A decade or so prior, NASA had sent plants on a mission for a study that concluded that indoor plants improved the air qual-ity in enclosed spaces. While they did not use Woolly Pockets for the experiment, it did validate the company's hypothesis.

This job showed me that I could have a slightly higher pur-pose for my work, and that a well-defined, mission-driven product—in this case, based on the belief that more plants make the world a better place—can be key to a successful company. When I joined in 2010, I was the sole employee at our office in L.A. and we only sold product online. By 2012, we had thirty employees and were selling to two hundred and fifty stores across the world.

We launched a school garden initiative, and I started traveling around the country trying to talk administrators and parents into letting us install school gardens using Woolly Pockets, my first foray into America's highly complex educational system. That was how I learned that because of a recent law, public schools were obligated to serve a nutritious breakfast and lunch to kids, and without charge to those who came from low-income families. But then I also learned that some schools spend less than two dollars a day per kid for food, which explains why Tyson and Nabisco, two huge perpetrators in factory farming and processed foods, provide meals for children. We're feeding our kids empty calories. To make matters worse, in many states, it is illegal to feed kids vegetables grown on school grounds. Helping children develop a positive relationship to food felt personal to me.

I wanted to get Woolly Pockets to those states where it was possible to teach kids how to grow nutritious food, and so I cold-called principals all throughout the United States. One who stands out was a principal of a high school in South Central L.A. who wanted to try it with the kids kept after school for detention. I went with my colleague Becky, a blonde who wore glitter around her eyes and dressed entirely in vintage. The school "yard" was a concrete slab surrounded by a chain-link fence, with two basketball courts, neither of which had nets. Fifteen towering teenage boys were waiting for us in front of a graffitied wooden structure, none of them remotely interested in plants, or us.

I started my spiel: "All we need is a sunny spot, access to water, and an abandoned wall," I added, pointing to the structure.

"That is where we play handball," one boy said. I started to question what we were even doing there. Who were we to say they needed a garden?

But I pushed that thought aside, and Becky and I started nailing the pockets to the wall and filling them with soil as the boys watched. We planted tomatoes, red peppers, jalapeños, and cucumbers, as well as parsley, cilantro, and thyme. No one offered to help, or even feigned interest. After we were done, we left a few watering cans.

"Give them a drink every so often," Becky said.

No response.

In the car, we decided to laugh instead of cry. "Well, that was a dud!"

I was used to it: I had traveled to over a dozen states visiting schools and planting gardens. That was how I learned that many American parents considered ketchup a vegetable. By then, I had also begun flying to New York regularly to launch guerrilla gardening projects on blighted blocks and abandoned corners. It was always a flash event: I'd show up with a hundred Woolly Pockets and a U-Haul filled with all types of native varieties of zone-appropriate plants that would thrive with little to no maintenance. There were no permits, just plants. It gave me flashbacks to being a child in Canada with my mom, throwing seed bombs out of the window and then watching them bloom.

On one trip, Miguel had a particular spot in mind, across from the Standard Hotel in the Meatpacking District of Manhattan. Once there, I noticed this tall, lanky blond man who looked like he was about to go on safari, in khaki shorts, a button-up shirt, and socks pulled up to his knees. His name was Mark and a friend of mine from L.A. had recommended that we hire him to help install plants.

"He has a green thumb," she explained.

He also had a distinct style, and I particularly liked his shoes: suede ankle boots with a rubber sole. They were so well worn that I could see where the laces had rubbed away the suede to a dull shine. The best type of fashion, I believe, are those items that tell that person's story.

"Ooh, cool shoes," I said.

"They're veldskoens," he said in his thick South African accent.

"What are veldskoens?" I asked, amazed there was a type of shoe that I had not yet heard of.

He explained that the word was Afrikaans and directly translated to "field shoe." The original version simply involved wrapping feet in rawhide leather to protect against South Africa's desert-like terrain. A rubber sole was added later. The design had since evolved to three pieces of leather sewn and held in place with rivets and canvas-like shoelaces. Most South Africans, Mark explained, called them "Vellies," pronouncing the V like an F.

"It is said in South Africa that the only things that can survive the apocalypse are cockroaches and veldskoens," Mark said with a smile.

As we worked through the night, making a magical garden, Mark told me that he had grown up wearing these shoes as a kid in South Africa. He knew a guy who had a workshop down the road from his grandparents' house in Namibia.

Vellies made me think of the mukluks and kimonos my mother cherished. They also reminded me of the Clarks desert boots Rastafarians liked to wear in Jamaica, but were more rustic and handmade, less manufactured. Back in L.A., I did some research and learned that the British first saw that shoe during their ravaging of Africa. They brought it back to the U.K., where Clarks, the British shoe company, copied the design, called it a "desert boot," and has since made a fortune.

Meanwhile, Woolly Pockets was thriving: We were up to several million in sales and could afford full-page ads in *The New York Times*. It was around this time that the principal from that South Central L.A. school called me. "The guys want to show you something," he said. "Can you come back here?" Becky and I went the next day, a bit nervous. But when we arrived, we were thrilled to see that the garden was thriving, and those same kids were beaming.

"I told my dad about this garden," one said. "Turns out my granddad was a farmer."

"I did not know that our ancestors lived off the land," another said. "Planting is meaningful. Farming is a tool of empowerment, freedom, and self-sufficiency."

They decided to make salsa out of the tomatoes, onions, ja-

lapeños, and cilantro they grew, and it was so good, they started
selling it at their local farmer's market. My heart was brimming.
This felt really good.

My relationship with Miguel, however, was tricky. His ec-
centricity sometimes bordered on maniacal. And while I believed deeply in the company mission, I was not making enough
money considering how much of my heart and soul I poured
into my work.

Miguel was also very big on the concept of company culture, and my job was to help cultivate it. I made sure that all the
employees took time out to have lunch together every day, and
we made a vocab list of "woolly words," the suggestion being
that every employee had to include two in each email. "Plantas-
tic" was Miguel's favorite. Others included "ethereal," "sensory," "grow." The concept was that if you are forced to put
these words in your emails, you had to consider: "What am I
communicating? How is it making the recipient feel? And how
is it furthering our mission?"

Miguel was also hosting what he called Secret Suppers,
invite-only three-course dinners. I never attended, but I heard
rumors about one where naked people were on swing sets hanging from the ceiling and cotton candy was served as an appe-
tizer. The final course was raw meat, by which point people
were having sex on the table—at our office. (It should come
as no surprise that Miguel was one of the early Burning Man
festivalgoers.)

The office culture was hard for me to swallow, but the straw
that broke the camel's back for me was when Miguel announced,
"We need a viral video."

The concept of viral videos was relatively new in 2010; a popular example was a five-second video from a few years before called "Dramatic Chipmunk." Suspenseful music played, the camera zoomed in, and a prairie dog (not even a chipmunk) turned its head to the camera. That was it. The concept of viral anything was still nascent, but even then, I was pretty sure it could not be premeditated, at least not by Miguel.

But he was insistent. "Let's hire an ad agency!" he said. "I want to do the dramatic squirrel thing, but with a plant and a gnome."

Meanwhile BP's gargantuan oil spill was still fresh in everyone's mind. In April 2010, the Deepwater Horizon oil rig exploded in the Gulf of Mexico, killing eleven people and dumping 200 million gallons of oil into the ocean. That spring and summer, we were all bombarded with images of oil-slicked birds and turtles and tar-ball-littered beaches, and story after story of the environmental damage done. I was working on a project that would use plants to render a BP gas station useless for a few days—to show nature fighting back against this man-made horror show. It was a project that felt so much more connected to the mission of this company. I was also working eighteen-hour days, sometimes seven days a week, to the point where I had no time for Fresh. Our still new relationship was feeling the strain, and to see Miguel making big financial decisions that felt so off to me made me realize that this was not my path.

At that point, we only had enough in the marketing budget to choose either a hyper-lapsed video of a massive guerrilla gardening project protesting BP using Woolly Pockets, or a clip mimicking a chipmunk but using a garden gnome.

The forty-thousand-dollar budget was equivalent to my salary, and the guerrilla-gardening video was a no-brainer for me. From a value standpoint and a viral-possibility standpoint, it made all the sense in the world. But Miguel wound up hiring an agency to make a gnome video. That was my cue: It was time for me to go and do my own thing. I did not know yet where or what that would be. But I felt sure I would find it.

11

wanderlust

It was the summer of 2010, and it was obvious that Fresh and I were chasing different things: I wanted to make and save money and focus on my career. Fresh was interested in making graffiti and spending any money he did make as quickly as he got it.

"Goals are for people who want to get caught in the trap," he often said.

To him, that trap was capitalism, and he was uninterested. I thought of something my mom often said as I grew up: "If you are not a socialist in your twenties, you have no heart. But if you're not a capitalist in your thirties, then you have no brain."

We amicably agreed to split. I was in my mid-twenties and ready for a change of scenery and decided to move to New

York. I was not sure what my next career move would be, but I knew I had a better chance of discovering it there. I found an apartment in Bed-Stuy on Craigslist and moved in, sight unseen. I also started dating a photographer I had met on a Woolly Pocket shoot named Jason. He was from Kansas and six feet tall with blond hair and blue eyes. Super kind and soft-spoken with a slight stutter, he was an assistant to several fashion photographers, including Steven Meisel and Ruven Afanador. Jason was talented, hardworking, and deeply immersed in fashion, and his ambition matched my own.

I knew my savings would not last long, so I cold-emailed a casting director named Jennifer Starr and started assisting her on Ralph Lauren, Gap, and Calvin Klein campaigns to pay my rent. It meant long hours in a big city, but I loved every moment of it.

I also agreed to do freelance work for Gen Art again connecting up-and-coming designers with sponsors to create shows during New York Fashion Week. That sometimes meant visiting stores like Opening Ceremony and scouring social media and blogs in search of young creative talent who would benefit from support. Started in 2002 by Carol Lim and Humberto Leon, Opening Ceremony had quickly become the nexus of all fresh new designers in New York. During one store visit, I asked Olivia Kim, their first employee, which new designers she was excited about. She pulled a few well-cut denim pieces in exaggerated shapes off the racks along with baby tees and cropped jackets with big utilitarian pockets. The look felt like New York City worker meets Candy Land. I was all in.

The Okpo sisters, Lizzy and Darlene, had just launched a

brand called William Okpo, named for their Nigerian father. I asked Olivia for their number and the next day, two stunning women, with box braids that nearly swept the floor, arrived at my Bed-Stuy apartment dressed in a mix of vintage and their own brand. They had grown up in all five boroughs of New York City, knew the subway better than anyone I had ever met, and were passionate about what they were making and doing.

But as I flipped through their look book, I had to disguise my disappointment. The photographs and graphic design did not even come close to capturing the vibrant women sitting on my couch, or their designs. The lighting was not right, the models did not show the clothes well. Plus, there was not one photo of the two of them together. Creating imagery for a brand is expensive. You need a stylist, a photographer who has lights and a studio, and models who know how to actually sell the attributes of a garment. These sisters had no shortage of creativity, only a shortage of resources. I knew they would have a hard time going up against the Alexander Wangs of the world, whose parents had tons of resources to back their launches.

So I sprang into action. Jason and I were living together by then, and the following week he took a stunning photo of the sisters in our apartment and reshot their look book there too. My friend Ashleah was an agent at Society agency and sent an incredible new model who was excited to work with Jason and support new young designers. Jason worked with assistants to well-known makeup artists and hairdressers, which was how Kanako, Pat McGrath's right hand, came to help. We were all working for free, happy to be doing it, knowing there is an unspoken bond and barter economy among a certain type of young creative person in New York that ensures all ships will rise with the tide.

Meanwhile, I was still thinking of what I wanted to do. Freelance fashion work was a great way to get my feet wet and pay rent, but I was still searching for what would drive me. I was also experiencing an intense pull toward Africa.

My mom had somehow acquired a time-share in Marrakesh. She still loved traveling when she could, and passed that wanderlust on to me. Jason and I saved two thousand dollars and went for two weeks. It was my first trip to a continent that felt so big to me, emotionally and physically. I had been thinking more and more about my father, and my own Ghanaian roots.

Morocco was sensory overload: Beautiful shades of terra-cotta, mustard yellows, warm browns, sky blues, and sage greens kaleidoscoped with the intoxicating smells of cinnamon, cumin, turmeric, and peppermint. Add the brass and metal elements—from doorknobs and knockers to bells and belts— and I was like a kid in a candy store. It was different from anywhere I had been before.

I could, and would, sit for hours in different carpet sellers' stalls as exquisitely designed rugs were unfurled in front of me, each from a different region, time period, or group of artisans. Some were simple white lambswool with brown diamond shapes, others had bright red backgrounds with purple, orange, and yellow patterns. Each told a very specific story, which the sellers would excitedly share as they poured me mint tea, giddy to have a visitor as eager to understand the cultural history of these items as they were to tell it.

It was also here where I fell in love with the babouche. I first

noticed the slipper-like shoe when I saw a group of men scurry-
ing into a mosque in the medina, the marketplace at the city's
epicenter. These men, elegantly dressed in their djellabas and
caftans, would quickly slip off their shoes before going in to
pray. I looked at the lines of soft leather slippers and saw that
the back heels were all pushed down, as if they had been stepped
on. It made sense: Muslims pray throughout the day, so they
need a shoe they can slip on and off with ease. I thought about
all the items my mother had collected over the years, how often
clothing had a purpose that extended well beyond its beauty.
When form and function marry, something as simple and beautiful as the babouche is born.

I started looking for the shoes everywhere, in the markets
and shops, on people. Often, I could see the back heel was
steamed down, giving it a mule-like effect. Some, however,
were sewn or glued down. On the streets flashier versions were
trendy, but I was drawn to the sun-faded suedes that were dyed
naturally, creating dusty rose and terra-cotta hues. I began buying pairs, not even checking to see if they would fit me. I simply
wanted to appreciate them. No two were identical as each pair
was handmade, and yet, they all shared the same easy-on-and-
off effect. I loved the way a person's daily rituals would become
blended into their wardrobe, so that little style details become
ingrained in a culture, handed down from ancestors. Proof of
life and a rite of passage.

Of course, among the babouche, Moroccan rugs, copper
teapots, and mosaic tiles for sale in the medina, there were also
a lot of Ed Hardy T-shirts and True Religion jeans. Western
influence was always seeping through. But before we left Mo-

rocco, I traveled deep into the medina in search of the babouche craftsmen themselves, to watch them meticulously cut and sew. I asked one of my favorite vendors for his contact info to keep in touch. I had the vague idea that I might open a store in the East Village to sell a variety of things that I discovered during my travels, like the babouche.

Back in Brooklyn, I wore my babouche around the house and to get coffee in the neighborhood and started to think about what design elements I might want to change to adapt the shoe to New York City life. I began sketching in a notebook, taking some of my babouche apart and making tweaks so that they hugged the foot a little bit better. I added additional padding to the insole and even toyed with adding a heavier outsole too. As I sketched, I realized that this modified babouche was precisely the type of thing I wanted to offer in my dream store. So I reached out to the Marrakesh vendor and requested he make me a special pair out of denim. He asked me to send him material, and I responded, "Can you find an old pair of jeans and use those?"

The first pair was not quite right, and I asked for more tweaks, communicating via WhatsApp with my sketches and mediocre high school French. He sent four or five different samples, every pair a slight variation, as he was working to find what he thought I meant. Each one got a little closer to what I envisioned. I finally asked him to place the denim seam down the center of the shoe. He did, and I did not know it then, but that would become a prototype of my first Brother Vellies shoe.

·   ·   ·

A few months later, the Okpo sisters asked me to come with them to Nigeria. Their first-ever fashion show through Gen Art was such a huge success that they were now fielding invitations to attend others, including Arise Fashion Week in Lagos. I had been working with them as a friend/free consultant, helping with pricing and press opportunities, and I desperately wanted to see their business grow. They were immensely talented and deserved to make a living off their creative work. This event seemed like a good opportunity for them to gain exposure in a new market, which also happened to be where their family was from.

Despite their obvious talent, they struggled to break through in an industry that still felt elitist and classist: They did not have a Central Saint Martins or Parsons degree, nor an internship at Carolina Herrera. And to gain access to some of the most talented seamstresses and patternmakers remained virtually impossible without a lot of funding and big retailers backing you. So the Okpo sisters' samples were made by people they could find, not the fancy sample makers who'd trained at ateliers and worked at Calvin Klein for decades. And without a solid team that really prioritizes you, on-time production is impossible. This combination made it incredibly difficult for the sisters to succeed in the hyper-demanding and competitive fashion world.

They asked me to come on full-time, and while I was eager to help them, I knew I couldn't work for other people anymore. I was still searching for what my own personal project would be. However, I was happy to help the Okpo sisters as a freelancing friend—and eager to return to Africa.

. . .

Arise Fashion Week was sponsored by *Arise* magazine, "Africa's global style and culture magazine," owned by a Nigerian media mogul, Nduka Obaigbena. I was excited to attend, and still determined to visit every corner of that continent in search of the energy and familiarity I'd found in Morocco. I know in some way, I was also looking for traces of my father.

Lagos is often portrayed as the dazzling financial capital of Africa, so I was surprised to arrive at an airport that felt straight out of the 1970s, with water leaking from the ceiling, no air-conditioning, and a luggage conveyor belt that lurched forward in a way that was painful to watch.

As soon as the sisters and I exited baggage claim, a man approached us and said he was our driver. It was early evening, and we were desperate to get to our hotel.

We got in the car, and we were about to leave when I said, "What about the models? Are you getting a car for them?" I saw one girl get off the plane who looked to be seventeen years old and totally on her own. I knew there was a thin line between modeling and sex trafficking, and so I was concerned for her safety.

He said, "No, they can find their own way." Then sped off. I was on high alert from then on.

The fashion week was supposed to be in full swing, but when we got to the hotel, we learned that the event was delayed, and that the Wi-Fi was not functioning. I was still working for Gen Art and needed to get work done. By then, we had been traveling for sixteen hours and were tired and starving. We decided to regroup after we had a meal and a good night's sleep. But when we went downstairs, the hostess informed us that they had run out of food.

"What do you mean?" I asked.

"But not to worry," she said with a smile that made it clear that this fact was not going to change so I should focus my efforts elsewhere. I once again thought of the models stranded at the airport.

"Has anyone gone to pick up the models?" I asked.

"A car is on its way," she reported. "But unfortunately, there is no hotel room for them."

"Where will they stay?" I asked, panic replacing worry.

The hostess shrugged.

The next day, we heard rumors that one of the models was held at gunpoint the night before. We also learned that the show had been delayed by several days. The sisters had commitments in New York that they would have to cancel in order to stay in Nigeria, so we weighed our options. They were one of the headliners of the event and meant to make several appearances. The next morning, we informed the organizer that we would do the show, but then would have to leave the following day and not stay for the other events.

She was furious: "You should be grateful for the opportunity," she fumed.

With only two days in Lagos, we decided to make the most of it. We went to the market, which, to be expected, had a completely different vibe from the one in Marrakesh. It felt authentically Nigerian, and less of a tourist hustle. I wandered through the labyrinth of tiny stalls squashed together, each selling something made locally, including gorgeous baskets, textiles, wood carvings, snakeskins, and animal pelts. The smell of suya roasting over the fire filled the air alongside the joyful chitter-chatter of the vendors and shoppers. I heard the Lijadu Sisters' music being blasted from a boom box propped up on a small wooden stool, just as four cats slinked by and jumped up onto huge rolls of lace, in fluorescent colors. Surprised, I went to investigate and saw that the lace was machine-made in China. I remembered the conversations I'd had with my mother when we went vintage shopping, and specifically that Nigeria was known for its handmade lace. I asked that vendor where I could find the authentic version of the synthetic material he was selling. He scrunched up his face and said, "Nowhere that I know of," with a shrug. That made me wonder what other Nigerian art forms and artisans had been displaced because of cheaply made imported products.

As I continued to wander through the market, I noticed that the booths selling handmade soaps or fresh herbal teas or really any kind of handmade product were less trafficked than those selling Chinese plastics in bright, eye-catching colors. I also noticed that the people working in the stalls were dressed in American T-shirts, some with typos, rather than in the traditional Nigerian clothes they were selling. I recalled my conversation with the thrift store worker in L.A. and wondered if this was the impact our hand-me-downs were having. I had the sense that the remaining makers of beautifully handcrafted Nigerian lace, indigo-dyed cotton, and other traditional materials were holding on by a thread.

We returned to the hotel that evening and I did not feel comfortable sleeping alone, so I moved into Lizzy and Darlene's room. The next morning, we did the show, which went fine. Still, we were eager to get back to Brooklyn, and had planned to do so the next day.

That night, after we'd all drifted asleep, we were jolted awake by a loud banging on our door at one A.M. We cracked it open and saw an extremely tall African man wearing a kente cloth and matching hat and flanked by security guards. It was Nduka, the Nigerian mogul who owned the Arise empire.

"I heard you want to leave!" he said as he barged into the room, uninvited, and sat on the couch, across from me and the sisters, who were now huddled on opposite sides of me on the bed. I could feel their bodies tense up. Suddenly, I felt as though I was dealing with my stepfather. I felt the need to protect the sisters.

"You cannot leave!" he said. "You signed a contract!"

He had large square teeth that sat beneath an overgrown mustache, whose wayward hairs stretched into his mouth when he spoke.

I stayed steady. I knew that I could not waver with people who usually got their way through intimidation. I knew I had to be matter-of-fact. Also, there was no contract.

"We have other engagements in New York," I said flatly. "We don't have a choice but to leave."

The air felt still and heavy in our windowless room.

We had done everything we'd agreed to do. We had dressed the models and done the fashion show already. It was not our fault the show was postponed. We had delivered our part of the equation and he had not. It was that simple. Still, I knew better than to argue.

"Well, how will you get home?" he countered, with a snicker.

A chill ran down my spine. I told him we would continue the conversation in the morning and somehow managed to get him to leave our room. As soon as the sun cracked a bright orange line in the dark morning sky, we took a cab to the airport and boarded the first flight back to New York.

I was happy to be home, and yet, I did not want to let my Arise experience temper my growing curiosity to learn more about the continent my father was from. I had more exploring to do. I also kept thinking about veldskoens, and how cool it would be to do an update of that shoe, like I had done with the babouche. My thought was that I could sell both shoes to fashion-conscious people who were, like me, interested in the cultures where the shoes originated and would like to support the people in those places who made the shoes. The more I thought about it, the more excited I became.

I wanted to find a workshop in Namibia or South Africa that was already making veldskoens, and then work with the shoe-makers there to update and refine the design for a Western audience. It felt like a more holistic and sustainable way to support the local community, in stark contrast to what Clarks did. I wanted to provide a beautiful and meticulously made product to people who liked the shoe shape and to teach them a bit about the culture it came from at the same time.

But finding workshops where veldskoens were made was hard: A Google search led me to random people's travel blogs that might mention a small place in a rural town where they had bought a pair. These shoes seemed to exist only as part of the local economy, made in small local workshops. So I reached out to Mark, who offered to connect me to the workshop where he had gotten the shoes he was wearing the first time I met him. He even proposed going with me, and then Jason decided to come, too, as we both knew the trip would warrant photographs.

We flew into Windhoek, the capital of Namibia, which was much sleepier than Lagos. It was a curious city, adjacent to a natural hot spring and littered with German castles. The sun shone brightly and warm air coming in from the Kalahari Desert danced across my skin. After a quick lunch of mahangu fish soup and oysters, we rented a car and prepared to drive four hours to a town on the west coast called Swakopmund. Jason, Mark, and I took turns driving a Nissan Sentra across a rugged desert landscape so riddled with potholes that our tire popped within the first two hours. After replacing the tire, we made it to the tiny coastal town later that afternoon. It was quiet and quaint and the sun reflected a sequence of dancing diamonds off the ocean.

We finally drove down a long, windy road and arrived at a small cement building, roughly eight hundred square feet. Inside, seven men were working, a group of mainly Ovambo and Herero men with two Himba—you could tell by their four front bottom teeth, which were missing, strategically extracted. I learned from Mark that this was part of their own personal decoration, much like how we put on braces to straighten our teeth. All the artisans were standing at individual tables handcutting rawhide with scissors.

Namibia is one of the last places where the Herero people live, and it was incredible to see the women in town. They stood out in their colonial-style, formal-looking gowns—which were corseted with layers of petticoats—which spoke to a history of what had happened here, but the way that they chose to presently embody that style of dress, using colorful African textiles, was subversive and striking. They also wore a headpiece that was meant to pay homage to cows, called a otjikava, which is typically fashioned from newspaper, shaped to mimic cow horns, and then covered with fabric to match the dress. I was awestruck.

I started asking them questions—some knew English, though there were four or five different languages spoken in the space. Mark did a bit of translating and I learned that all the leather for the shoes was sourced from local farmers who participated in a government-mandated culling of kudu, a deerlike animal that, due to climate change, had become so overpopulated they had started infringing on the farmland and eating fruits and vegetables, which impacted the food supply for families. It functioned as a natural ecosystem: An allotted number of kudu were killed to maintain a healthy population size, the meat was eaten, and the hide was used to make items to clothe the community—including shoes. I was fascinated and wanted to understand everything about the process.

Next, I went to the tannery. I had been a vegan for almost a decade by then, and had continued to watch documentaries and read reports about the abysmal way animals can be treated. So I was nervous, but I was also reminded that when an animal, farmer, and community are in sync, it can be a beautiful relationship. I was also starting to grapple with the idea that a lot of my own veganism was a transference of my earlier eating disorders. Of course, I found great meaning in the environmental impact of veganism. But for me, it was ultimately also a great cover for an unhealthy quest to control my body and be unnaturally thin. But I also did not want to support the way meat is processed and sold in the United States. In Namibia, it was a very different method and ethos: Who was I to criticize or even comment on the relationship Namibians had to the animals they ate?

On my drive to the tannery, I saw kudu out and about. When we arrived, I also saw their pelts being harvested and processed, and already knew that every part of each animal killed was being used. I also understood that I could not judge these choices that made sense for this community. A vegan way of being would be next to impossible and entirely unpractical for Namibians. And yet, I realized that back in the United States, I would run up against a specific breed of culturally insensitive vegans and animal rights advocates who opposed these practices.

I was already thinking about how I could bring these shoes to America. Despite my personal beliefs, it made no sense to import "vegan leather" or faux furs to make Vellies. Both were made almost entirely out of plastic known to shed tiny pieces into our environment in the same way our skin sheds cells. These microplastics wreak havoc as they float in the air and permeate the water. Studies have found evidence of this in our lungs, as well as proof that there are more microplastics in the ocean than stars in the sky. Still, I knew that PETA and other animal rights activists would come at me for using fur and leather. So I stopped referring to myself as vegan. That did not mean I started eating meat or dairy; I simply did not want to associate myself with the type of groupthink that did not make sense outside of a specific sliver of America.

I also knew that using kudu would be a complicated proposition. Most people believe cows provide the best type of leather, and I imagined the American imagination running wild with images of *The Lion King*. Meanwhile, cows are a rare commodity in southern Africa—the Nguni people named themselves after the cow they lovingly farm. For them, killing a cow is not taken lightly.

As with the babouche, I knew that with a few tiny design tweaks I could make the Vellie more fashion-forward and coveted by the American market. I wanted to first make a pair of shoes for myself, completely by hand, to learn the process. I asked the artisans at the workshop if they were open to teaching me, and they happily agreed. I headed back to the tannery to select my first hide. As I ran my hand across the smooth suede and leather kudu, I spotted a heavier, darker hide from an oryx, which is a huskier and taller antelope-like creature with silvery gray fur and dark brownish-black stripes at the base of its belly that extend down its legs. I took it back to the workshop and sat with the guys there, who enthusiastically taught me every step of the shoemaking process. First, I used the pattern pieces to trace onto the hide where I wanted to take each piece of the shoe, and then I cut out the leather with a blade. The positioning was artful and important. I decided to use the section of the hide where the bullet had entered on the heel, my way of acknowledging that I was wearing a real animal that experienced a very real death.

So often, especially in fashion, we discard or dismiss the ugly parts of things. But those parts have value. For me, using that part of the leather reminded me that the material represented life, and what we do with it matters. And how we price and pay for it also matters because it will affect how the animals and the land are treated. If your farmers cannot afford to eat, rest assured that their animals won't be eating either.

The men who were teaching me showed me how to use a metal spike to punch holes in the leather where the laces would go. I slowly and carefully sewed the pieces to form the shoe myself, with their guidance. They gathered around me, watching me stitch inch by inch. Then I traced my own foot onto a particularly beautiful piece of leather they used for the insole.

"It feels so good!" I said.

At the end, I attached the rubber sole with glue and marveled at the shoe fully formed on its carved wooden last. My eyes drifted back to the gorgeous offcuts we used for the insole leather. I recognized that it was the same leather used for Louis Vuitton handles: the rawest kind, vegetable tanned, which slowly patinas over time from human touch or sunlight.

That was an aha moment for me: All these artisans were using the same kind of leather to make beautiful products—the only difference was that it was Himba hands versus Italian, Black versus white. Celebrated versus forgotten.

I was very proud of my first pair of handmade Vellies! And making the shoes myself helped me understand how important the process was, specifically how many people were needed to make the shoe—from the farmer who killed the animal to the tanner who cured the hide to the artisans who carefully and thoughtfully produced each pair of shoes by hand. I knew that this could never be a mass-market product that would sell for sixty bucks. It also made me think about how expensive things really are and need to be.

I still wear that shoe, with the bullet-hole heel, to this day.

I wound up making a bunch of shoes from that oryx hide. I also bought a few other kudu hides and asked the Himba women to dye several with the red ochre pigment they use every day to color their bodies and hair. In leather, it turns a red with brown undertones.

The women cover their entire bodies with otjize, which is made of butter fat and ochre pigment. It protects their skin from the harsh Namibian elements and tints their skin a reddish brown. It is considered beautiful and highly desirable in their culture. They also use the otjize to encase long strands of their hair, and the effect is a stunning sculptural crown of reddish-brown clay-like strands.

I came back from Namibia with a dozen shoes packed carefully in my luggage and immediately applied for a stall at the Hester Street Fair on New York's Lower East Side. A week later, I was approved for a stall on Saturday mornings, which cost seventy dollars to rent. I printed fifty postcards with photos of the artisans that Jason had taken in Namibia, and laid them out next to the Vellies we had for sale. This was my litmus test: Would people be interested in buying and wearing these shoes?

Truthfully, I had sunk my entire thirty-five hundred dollars savings into that trip. My account was in the negative. I needed this to work.

Watching people try them on in real time was invaluable. I was just learning about shoes and so understanding fit issues and receiving customer feedback were important. People often compared the shoes to desert boots or Clarks, which was my opportunity to tell the story of the Vellies. That first Saturday, I sold three pairs of shoes. I was elated.

One Saturday, a reporter from *The New York Times* Style section stopped by. She had visited the week before anonymously and purchased a pair of red veldskoens. On her second visit, she brought her notebook and said that she wanted to do a story on these Vellies.

"Have you thought of building a website?" she asked. "These shoes are amazing—and people are going to want to buy them!"

She was right. And when her article came out a week later, the tiny Shopify template site I had managed to construct with my friend sold out.

That planted a seed.

I gave Lizzy and Darlene each a pair, as well. They were working at Opening Ceremony to help pay their bills and showed them to the store founders, Humberto and Carol, who loved the shoes and the story behind them. They asked me to design a collection for their store. It was my first official order!

Like the babouche, I altered the veldskoen shape and made it more contemporary—narrower and more elegant than the original slightly boxy, rough-hewn shape. I updated the rivets and eyelets, switching from silver to recycled brass. I went back to Namibia and worked with the artisans, who taught me about natural dyes and what can be accomplished in the tanning process, where they lay the skins out in the sun to dry—the longer they bake, the darker the patina. Instead of chemicals, we experimented with baobab and avocado oils, and massaging different flower pigments with shea butters. Being both a vegan and my mother's daughter, I had been experimenting with natural oils and butters for years—in my cooking, for medicinal reasons, and also as beauty products. Shea butter lip balms mashed with my favorite lipstick colors; honey and moringa oil face masks; drenching my hair in castor oil for an hour spent sitting in the sun. So it was incredible for me to have the opportunity to work directly with farmers who grow, harvest, and utilize these abundant gifts from nature in their own way.

During that visit, I saw the entire process. One guy's sole job was to watch the leather dry, which could take a week or more. I started to wonder, "If so many women are willing to wait for a Birkin bag to be made in France, would they also be willing to wait for this incredible shoe?"

On that trip, I stayed for two weeks while the shoes were being made and asked the shoemakers to discreetly include parts of the leather usually discarded—the burr marks and scratches that occurred naturally on an animal that had enjoyed a life fully lived in the wild. I also included the bullet holes. No two shoes were alike. My whole life I'd loved shoes, but now I understood how they were made, and how they could be made for good.

To this day, everything I know about making shoes I learned in Africa.

. . .

I flew back to New York with one hundred pairs of shoes in my three checked bags. Once in my apartment, I carefully packaged each pair in recycled cardboard shoeboxes, hailed a taxi, and dropped them off at Opening Ceremony. Our classic Vellie sold for between $195 and $285. Our wholesale price was half that and the cost was half that, according to the norms of wholesale pricing—though many brands factor a lot of things into that wholesale price, which ends up minimizing the allocation for labor. I wanted to make sure our margins stayed healthy, and the artisans were properly paid.

The shoes sold well, especially to men, and we got another order from Opening Ceremony. I began to get more creative with the designs and started to envision something beyond selling items in a single retail store. I was learning about construction, sourcing, supply chains, margins, and pricing. Both the babouche and the Vellies were embraced by my trend-forward friends and I was growing more passionate about designing shoes that were made by the people who were connected culturally to that design. I thought, "This could be a company."

Opening Ceremony was still my only customer, but the shoes continued to sell. By then, *The New York Times* story had created such a demand I decided to sell Vellies on pre-order. Mark offered to oversee the production in Namibia, and since I was still working freelance to make ends meet, I agreed.

Mark left for Namibia in October. By December customers started asking, "Where are the shoes?" My communication with Mark was sporadic, but he never indicated there was an issue with production. We now had fifty customers waiting for the shoes they had already paid for, and some asked for their money back. That was when the accountant I had hired to help me with the company's finances called.

"Aurora, the company account has been drained," he said, sounding alarmed. "Every single dollar was withdrawn from an ATM in Namibia."

I began to panic. At that moment, all I knew was that Mark had disappeared, along with all the money that was needed to fulfill those shoe orders. I had to think fast. And maybe start over.

12

from Africa with Love

By then, I was committed to African artisans making high-end products and to creating a company that would reframe the narrative of hands of color participating in luxury fashion. Luxury, to me, meant more than interlocking letters forming a prestigious logo. It meant everyone in the supply chain getting paid fairly and being treated with respect.

I was still contemplating the fact that "made in Italy" or "made in Paris" was automatically seen as luxurious, as opposed to "made in China," which was immediately written off as fast and cheap. "Made in Africa" was an utterly foreign concept to people. I aimed to change that.

I made the tough decision to stop producing in Namibia, and I had to find a new workshop that could make fifty pairs of shoes—fast. Mark had introduced me to the Namibian workshop. I had no idea what happened over the course of his relationship with them, but I was devastated that we never received the shoes I had ordered. It was unclear whether he had ever given them the money in the first place.

It also concerned me that there was no government-mandated minimum wage in Namibia, which made it hard to know just how much the artisans were getting paid. A German factory owner promised me that he paid living wages, but he was unwilling to share the paperwork to prove it. I loved working with those artisans but knew I would meet others just as knowledgeable and talented. As much as I wished I could continue working with them, I also felt I needed a fresh start.

I had started an Instagram feed and began sharing both my travels and the shoes we were making. I wound up quickly finding my next workshop through a friend of a friend, who connected me with someone near Cape Town who knew about a workshop that had been making Vellies for generations.

"Let me go investigate," she said. "I will report back."

An hour later, she texted me a photo of a South African phone number scrawled across a napkin. I called it, and the man who answered introduced himself as John.

"Yes! We make that shoe," he said, equal parts eager and curious, with a thick South African accent.

I used my paycheck from Jennifer Starr to get back on a plane to visit his workshop the very next week with shoe orders that ranged from size one to fourteen, in all different colors. Vellies were such a wonderfully gender-neutral shoe that we were able to build on a singular sizing model. Vellies' size one was women's size five. Vellies' size five doubled as a traditional women's size nine and men's size seven. And so on. This allowed us to build less inventory and think beyond gendered norms from a design perspective, which was pretty unusual in 2013. The shoes were well made and utilized such high-quality leather that they wound up molding to your feet, which made our sizing model even easier for people to adopt.

John met me at his workshop and his jolly demeanor, accented by a glimmer in his eye and a full-throated laugh, put me at ease immediately. His family had been making Vellies in that small town for three generations, and he employed twenty highly skilled artisans, many of whom had been working for him or his father their whole lives. The workshop was a happy place, filled with laughter and music; Rodriguez or Simphiwe Dana would play throughout the day on a tiny radio with antennas. Light poured throughout the room and sometimes there was spontaneous dancing. It reminded me of the time I saw indigenous women making mukluks with my mom when I was young: a loving community making a living creating items directly related to their own culture and experience.

To fill the orders, we needed hides, so John drove me to several tanneries where I met a dozen farmers, some who only worked with kudu, others who raised ostriches. One man from the Nguni tribe raised the beautifully speckled Nguni cow, so sacred that the people are named for it, not vice versa.

I purchased two hides from him, which felt like a splurge as one cost the same as three kudu hides. We also visited a crocodile farmer who sold me two beautiful cognac-colored skins of South African hornback crocodile—named for the horn on the reptilian skin. I took the skins back to the workshop and made a single sample using the bumpy part of the horn on the front of the shoe and the spiky tail wrapped around the heel. I wanted to create items that were truly special, that honored the full life of the animal. I wanted to create future heirlooms.

The finished crocodile sample was gorgeous, and John explained that based on the way the horn was positioned, these shoes would be protective and virtually indestructible: African luxury with a wink to workwear. I was enamored with our new creation, which inspired me to call the farmer to ask how long it would take to get more crocodile skins.

"It could take three years," he said. "We don't kill the crocodiles! We wait for them to die." I laughed, of course. A reminder to slow my pace. Good things come to those who wait. But also, South African hornback shoes were not a scalable business model.

I knew I would find other possibilities, and started asking all the farmers I met: What else are you farming? What other materials are being thrown out? What is there not a local market for? What material do you save for special occasions? This was how I learned that, as with kudu, there was a mandated culling of springbok, another deerlike animal whose coat showcases a beautiful cascade of earthy tones, from deep blond to caramel, separated from its white underbelly by a dramatic dark brown swath. A man who made a biannual trip to John's workshop selling springbok hides agreed to come spend the afternoon teaching me about the animal and all the different ways its leather had been used by his tribe for generations. I started making samples with springbok and spent two weeks staying in a bed-and-breakfast down the street from the workshop. I flew back with duffel bags filled with a hundred shoes, including a tiny batch of patchworked kids' Vellies fashioned together from our leather offcuts. We were trying as best as we could to have zero waste.

Back in Brooklyn, I wrapped each shoebox in brown kraft paper and twine and piled them in a metal cart, which I rolled up Bedford Avenue to Sandbox Pack and Ship. There, Kariga, my favorite customer service guy, helped me ship each box individually. He was amused that I labeled each package, handwriting every customer's name and address with black Sharpie. "You know you can probably auto-generate mailing labels from your online store, right?" He winked knowing full well that I would never. This was a labor of love.

Now that I had found a new workshop, I could grow. I loved the energy there, and it felt important to me these South African shoemakers could earn a meaningful living by making an indigenous shoe. Clarks had made hundreds of millions of dollars based on the shape of the Vellie, and I wanted to see money go directly to this community for which the shoe had a clear history and relevance. John understood what was at stake, and that workshop was the main source of employment for many people in town. We discussed how vital it was—not to the individual artisans, but to the entire community. To keep the workshop alive, they had begun making a wide variety of Western-style shoes, but they greatly preferred the Vellie.

American consumerism has conditioned customers to want things at bargain prices—which has forced retailers and brands to continually try to get lower and lower pricing from the places that make the product. So most fashion companies make their shoes or clothes in factories in places like India, Bangladesh, and China. I thought of that documentary *Wal-Mart: The High Cost of Low Price*. The problem was that most of the CEOs and board members of those companies are unwilling to shoulder the financial burden of cutting costs themselves. Instead, they pass on those markdowns to the workshops, which means less pay and longer hours in unsafe working conditions for the workers, who more often than not are women of color. I wanted to disrupt that model by pricing items in a way that could ensure enough margin to pay the artisans fairly. I also decided we would try not to have sales—these shoes were worth the full asking price.

John was very supportive of that approach. He was also fully transparent: He told me about how much each shoe would cost to make. The South African rand was volatile, so I took their costs, factored in shipping and any other miscellaneous items, and made sure he was registered with the African Growth and Opportunity Act (AGOA), the preferential trade agreement the United States has with certain African countries, so we would not have to factor in the import duties. I added in packaging and a tiny bit of our operating costs, which allowed me to sell the Vellies for $265 and ensure the artisans were well paid for their products.

The idea of supporting this community through making and selling these shoes inspired the company name for me: Brother Vellies. I wanted to celebrate the brotherhood I was witnessing in this workshop as well as the larger community in South Africa who wore Vellies. They were a way of life. As ubiquitous as white Hanes T-shirts, Converse All Stars, or Levi's boot-cut jeans, classics that feel so distinctly American, wherever you see them in the world. I wanted Vellies to have that same connection to South Africa, beyond its borders.

"You really think your friends are going to like these shoes?" one of the shoemakers whispered to me one day while sanding down a tiny piece of displaced leather on a pair of nutmeg suede size sevens.

"No," I responded with a smile. "I think they're going to love them."

And I was correct. The orders kept coming. I was proving my hypothesis—that Vellies were a fashion proposition—and I was creating a steady stream of work for these artisans during a time when other traditional workshops were closing because they could not compete with cheap imports. And yet, whenever I told Americans that Vellies were made in Africa, they would inevitably say, "Like Toms?"

I would explain that we in fact made shoes in Africa and then sold them to anyone who wanted to buy beautifully crafted shoes. Toms makes their shoes in China, and then they give a pair to someone in Africa with every purchase. The company makes a profit on a charity mindset, and when it comes into a local community and gives away a thousand pairs of shoes, all those people who were making shoes for local markets potentially lose their jobs. Meanwhile, in all my travels to that vast continent, I had only ever seen Toms shoes on white tourists. These outside goods were killing local industries, and people needed jobs, not handouts. So even an order of a couple hundred pairs of Vellies made in South African workshops was a

game changer. This furthered my resolve that giving people opportunities to create their own well-being would be part of the
Brother Vellies mission.

Still, there were obstacles: South Africa was not producing
enough energy to support the country, so there were rolling
blackouts that would force the workshop to close as temperatures rose to a hundred degrees inside. Political unrest and
constant strikes made for volatile production and, at times, a
dangerous environment for everyone. There were also heavy
constraints around designing: Only one sole was available, one
style of rivet, one color of thread. Many of the artisans had not
been given the opportunity as children to learn how to read,
so I would hand-draw each design and color in every sample
sketch. To this day, I still send illustrated instructions, with as
few words as possible so that everyone at the workshops can
understand.

At this point, my goal was to raise awareness of the history
of Vellies so that we could continue to sell them and support
not only our workshop, but the whole artisan-made Vellie
community. I was not sure if Brother Vellies would ever be
more than that, and I still thought about opening a store in the
East Village, a place to sell both the Vellies and the babouche.

And I was still processing all of my travels across Africa: first
Morocco, then Nigeria, then Namibia, and now South Africa.
Kenya was next on my list. I wanted to explore what else I could
make in addition to shoes that supported local artisans and
economies. I knew Kenya had many different tribes who created jewelry using beads, carved wood, rope, brass, and bone, so
I flew to Nairobi on a research mission. From there, I made my

way up the east coast to a tiny town near Lamu, on the recommendation of a friend.

Kenya had a pace noticeably different from South Africa or Namibia. People walked and talked faster, and the answer to almost everything was "yes." Determination seemed to be a common trait, as everyone I met felt like they were eagerly awaiting opportunity.

The markets here were bustling with women carrying large baskets on their heads as tiny tuk tuk buggies whizzed by, sending chickens scrambling to get out of their way. Fruit stands overflowed with bright yellow mangoes and green guava, which gave the air a sweet scent that intermingled with the nutty scent of baobab seeds and smoky grilled chicken drenched in sugar syrup. Amid the sensory explosion, I saw a group of guys wearing traditional bright red plaid cloth wrapped around their bodies in a toga-like style that signaled they were from the Maasai tribe. One man wore an elaborate necklace that looked like a cascade of jangling silver coins and was attached to another line of coins that ran down his belly to a matching belt. Another wore a colorful strap with horsehair fastened below his knee, skirting his calf. Another had beautifully beaded ankle cuffs. It was precisely the type of artistry and craftsmanship that lured me in.

As I made my way over, I overheard them speaking very clear English with no accent. They were smoking cigarettes and had cellphones. Intrigued, I struck up a conversation and learned that only one of them was Maasai; the others were Kikuyu and had gone to university in Europe, but they told me they made more money being "fake Maasai" because tourists wanted to have an "authentic" experience, i.e., take photos and ask questions about their life and culture. The real Maasai didn't want to be bothered.

It was both humorous and amazing that these savvy college grads could offer this service, both to the tourists and the Maasai. Fashion's overuse of Maasai bodies had always bothered me: A white model jumping in a circle of Maasai men in a Valentino ad immediately comes to mind as an example of Black bodies being used as "exotic" props. I often wondered if, on photo shoots like that one, the Maasai were being disrupted from their lives in order to assist in the sales of an Italian-made handbag without being adequately compensated, but that begs a bigger question: What is adequate compensation for the appropriation of your culture?

I also noticed that the men were wearing sandals made from discarded safari vehicle tires that littered the Maasai Mara. I had spotted versions of them in the markets and even collected a few because I appreciated their ingenuity. They were Teva-like, which made me wonder what inspired that shoe. I particularly loved the brilliant reuse of the rubber that would otherwise be burned, releasing toxic chemicals into the clear Kenyan sky. They had not been given any of the infrastructure required to recycle the plastic, rubber, and petroleum-based goods imported by China and the United States.

I brought a few pairs back to South Africa and asked the artisans to make a sleeker version, using leather straps but maintaining the repurposed tire sole. I wanted to honor that part of the shoe, a great reuse of the discarded tires that freckled the coastlines and Saharan plains of East Africa.

They tried, but they couldn't get it right: The straps would sit too high or too low, cut too thick or too thin. It dawned on me that I was working with men who did not wear sandals, and I was asking them to make something that wasn't part of their culture. It wasn't intuitive to them, and they were struggling with it. That led to a clear realization: If I wanted to make Kenyan sandals, I needed to be making them in Kenya.

Travel to Africa is expensive, and I was still working as Jennifer Starr's assistant and as a freelance fashion producer while selling every Vellie that the new workshop produced. Moda Operandi reached out, wanting to sell them on their website, as did Olivia Kim, who had left Opening Ceremony for Nordstrom. By then, I had also designed a full line for kids, which *Vogue Italia* did a story on. *Vogue Paris* contacted me through Instagram and sent a photographer to my house to capture me at home with all my shoes.

I knew I was onto something. Brother Vellies was getting noticed. At this point, my apartment was my office and headquarters: I had an old rickety leather sewing machine and a ribbon press. I'd occasionally give myself a mini refresher in actual shoemaking, putting into practice what I had learned at the workshops. I started sewing not only with leather but taking apart my lesser loved jeans and worn-out jackets to create something new.

Brother Vellies had established a diverse client base, from artists like Mickalene Thomas to the guy who ran the corner bodega downstairs and came over religiously to try on new colors. Around that time, I was introduced to Chioma Nnadi, an editor at *Vogue,* at a William Onyeabor tribute performance at

BAM headlined by David Byrne, Dev Hynes, and the Lijadu Sisters. She asked about my "cool shoes," and I told her about Brother Vellies. That led to her emailing me in the spring of 2014 to ask: "Would you be interested in doing a travel journal for *Vogue*?"

I loved that idea for so many reasons: Selfishly, I was cash-strapped and knew that I could use that assignment to help cover the costs of my next trip as I could stay in hotels in exchange for writing about the experience. It was also an opportunity to share Brother Vellies with the *Vogue* audience and further prove my theory: Luxury goods could be made in Africa.

I said yes.

It was on this trip that I met Makeda, a formidable six-foot-tall dark-skinned woman with a broad smile and, like John, a twinkle in her eye. She was born and raised in a town not far from the Kenyan coast and ran a small workshop that made beaded sandals to sell to tourists. She employed a dozen local women and a few men who all worked in the same clay-and-brick workshop. I told her that she reminded me of John and his operation, and she was intrigued. "Tell me more about this John," she said, her eyes lighting up. I explained what we were doing in South Africa with Vellies, and how I wanted to do something similar with the sandals I had spotted in the local Kenyan markets. She immediately understood.

"I know how to make these shoes," she said, clearly interested.

When I told her about the design changes I wanted, she was not only game, but she also smiled and said, "Let's call them Tyre sandals."

Just as I had done in South Africa, I began looking for material to make samples. We went to a bustling fish market to source Nile perch, a fish skin thick enough to work as leather for shoes and bags. Jason came with me to take photos for *Vogue*, as well as for the Brother Vellies website and a batch of postcards that I would send to accessory editors asking for desk-side meetings, so they could see the collection in person when I returned. I found these more effective than cold emails.

I met goat farmers whose wives sheared the hair on hides into intricate patterns. Shearling inspired me to line the sandal insoles with the soft fluff, providing a breathable cloud beneath each step. Makeda suggested a trip to Nakuru, known for its chocolate-brown sheep whose time spent grazing in the high altitudes, close to the sun, created bleach blond tips. I loved how nature worked its own design magic; these were natural collaborations that people often tried to re-create quickly and cheaply in a factory with chemicals.

Makeda also took me to Kibera, the largest "slum" in Nairobi, to meet with artisans who had fallen on hard times without a sales outlet for their work. There I met a gentleman making brass pieces by melting padlocks. He was small in stature and had the creases of worry permanently etched in his face. I asked to see what else he was working on, and he gestured for me to follow him. We walked for twenty minutes through the labyrinthine sprawl before he led me through a tiny door revealing a small room covered with layers of glimmering thick white dust. There, he showed me beautiful beads that a friend of his had carved out of cow bones.

"Those are exquisite," I said.

The man smiled. "Thank you! I used to do this for American companies, but they wanted one order only before they left."

"Which companies?" I asked.

"They are called Anthropologies," he responded.

He saw my face scrunch up.

"Are they your friends?" he asked. "Do you know them?"

I was embarrassed. For myself as a person who had shopped there. For them. For fashion. For all of us complicit in creating an economy that valued profits over people. Designers loved the idea of doing capsule collections—small batches of products that were more "sustainable" or "inclusive" but only for a short time—to give themselves a halo of thoughtfulness before they quickly moved on, business as usual. I wanted to do it differently: I wanted to create meaningful long-term employment for these artisans.

When I first started talking about Brother Vellies as a sustainable luxury proposition, people were confused by the word "sustainable." And if they understood the concept, I was told it was boring. It was certainly not chic or sexy. I got it—most people think "sustainable fashion" is burlap bohemian, much like my mom dressed when I was growing up.

My idea of sustainable up to now was about creating beautiful things in beautiful ways, which meant working with local artisans, farmers, and gardeners in close proximity to one another in a way that took the fruit without eroding the soil. Not taking too much. Not forcing anything. And most important, making sure that things looked just as beautiful, if not more beautiful, when we left as when we first got there. If the community is an agricultural community that is farming and eating goat, then we work with what remains, the goat skin.

At the time, I did not know how big the market would be, but I knew there would be some people like me who cared. I also believe that people are inherently good and when presented with the opportunity to buy something that benefits everyone involved in making the product, as well as the environment, they will. And I also knew that the only way I was inspired to work was in a sustainable, thoughtful manner. I knew I would not get it right 100 percent of the time, but I was committed to trying to do better.

It is a lot smarter to build a company from the ground up with strong value propositions. If a founder is genuinely concerned about their environmental impact, being sustainable will come naturally. If a founder values the opinions and contributions of women, people of color, and other diverse categories of people, then they will be much more likely to have an inclusive brand and board.

Too often companies fail at reverse engineering their own value propositions. Simply because they weren't built with any values. It is not in their fiber. And in order for that to become ingrained in them, they have to ingest it. And for too many CEOs, values are a tough pill to swallow.

The *Vogue* diary that Jason and I shot was published in May 2014. The diary was such a gift because it allowed me to share

the Brother Vellies story by showing what we were doing instead of telling. It gave us an elegant platform to showcase beautiful images of those bone beads, the Nile perch, and the women
in Makeda's workshop. At that point in time, I could basically
name all our customers who made purchases on our website,
and 50 percent of them were repeat buyers. Brother Vellies was
building a customer base of people who loved these shoes and
how they were made. But *Vogue*'s approval, I hoped, would fuel
even more sales.

Each shoe sold continued to have a ripple effect: A purchase
order of a hundred pairs of shoes at the prices we were paying
artisans in Kenya, which was more than what they were selling
similar things for at the local market, was significant. It meant a
livelihood for Makeda and the women who worked for her, and
that many more women could be hired.

However, the political situation remained unstable. Makeda
never directly mentioned it to me, but I read about the Westgate
mall shooting in Nairobi. The militant Islamic terrorist group
al-Shabab claimed responsibility for the attack that left sixty-
seven people dead. Yet I was determined to create new products
with the women in the workshop, many of whom were seeing
things change for the better in their own lives.

Still, I was surprised when on our next production trip, a
month later, Jason and I found bars installed on the inside of the
bedroom door at the Airbnb where we had stayed previously.

"What is going on?" I asked Makeda when I saw her later
that afternoon to drop off sketches and material.

"You should probably leave these here and then go stay
somewhere else," she said.

"Why?"

"Al-Shabab has been reported in these areas," she said bluntly, a worried look in her eyes. "They have been abducting tourists." That thought had never crossed my mind, but her obvious concern made me realize this was possible.

"They ask for a ransom," she added. "In Kenya, if you harm a tourist, you are punished by death—so they want to take out everyone who has seen them." Basically, by traveling to this town, we had unknowingly put everyone at risk.

She then told us that just the day before, several people had been beheaded less than twenty miles away. We drove back to the house, terrified. There, the groundskeeper told Jason and me that if anyone came on the property, do not call him for help.

"They will kill you and me, as well," he said, averting his eyes. He also told us that one of the fake Maasai guys we had befriended had been taken into custody for being complicit in some of these crimes.

Jason and I went directly into our room, latched the iron door closed, and lay in bed fully clothed. It was getting dark, and we agreed to not turn on the light. We would just wait it out until the morning. As we lay in the dark silence, I was listening to my rapid heartbeat and Jason's shallow breath when a twig snapped outside, followed by a rustling in the bushes. My whole body tensed up.

"It could just be an animal," Jason whispered.

We were trying to figure out where we could go the next day. Back to Nairobi? Home? We tried to make a plan, lying on our backs, watching the ceiling fan spin above us, until it stopped.

"Maybe a blackout?" I ventured meekly.

My stomach, already in knots, turned leaden.

"Draw the blinds open," I said quickly and quietly. "And then meet me in the closet." I wanted whoever might be out there to see our bed was empty and assume we had left.

Jason did not question me; he just slipped out of bed and hastily opened the shades. The moonlight poured through, casting a silvery glow on the tile floors, illuminating our path as we quickly crawled into the closet and huddled next to each other, hearts racing. I shut the doors, careful not to make any sound as the two wooden flaps met. This felt familiar—while I never had to literally hide from Winston, I knew to trust my instincts when it came to dangerous situations. Crouched in the closet together, we heard more rustling. I squeezed Jason's hands, closed my eyes, and hoped we would make it to sunrise.

The next morning, still curled up in the closet, we were startled awake by a voice outside, and the sound of sweeping. We unfolded our bodies and emerged into the room and saw the groundsman through the window. We asked if he, too, had lost electricity, and he looked perplexed.

"No," he said, shaking his head.

We went to see Makeda, and I gave her the final sketches and instructions for the Tyre sandal samples and then headed directly to the airport, where we used the last of our money, approximately six hundred dollars, to charter an eight-seat plane into the Maasai Mara. Up until that point, I had been entirely uninterested in going on a safari, but Makeda said that was the safest place for us to go while we waited for the collection of shoes to be completed by the workshop.

As we lifted off, I felt relief. I was finally able to catch my breath as I sank into my small, cracked leather seat. Flying over the savannah, I saw tiny dots in the distance that revealed themselves to be enormous elephants alongside giraffes roaming the landscape, and my heart skipped a beat. I thought back to all the times as a child, writing letters to my pen pals and imagining a version of Africa, more fairy tale than fact, where wildebeests grazed and meerkats scurried about. Looking out through the tiny airplane window, I understood it was real. This was it.

13
Garden of Good and Evil

The Tyre sandals were a hit.

They sold out at Moda Operandi's trunk shows and at Opening Ceremony, as well as on our little website. With so many orders coming in, I was able to hire my first employee, Samantha, in the summer of 2014. It was such an exciting time and felt like a dream coming true.

I had met a woman at a cocktail party who worked for a developer who owned the South Street Seaport, which had been badly hit by Hurricane Sandy. They were looking for ways to revitalize the neighborhood, and after several spirited conversations, she offered me a space on Fulton Street where I would pay a percentage of sales as rent. That meant I now had a storefront, which could double as an office. It would allow people to try shoes on in person (which meant they would no longer have to come to my apartment—hooray!).

And so in November 2014, after one last apartment photo shoot for Meghan Markle's blog, The Tig, I moved Brother Vellies from my Bed-Stuy living room into what was an abandoned Ann Taylor store that still had flood lines on the wall from Hurricane Sandy. The Okpo sisters took the space next door.

Thanks to all the press coverage Brother Vellies had gotten, I had a surge of inquiries and a few other retailers interested in placing orders but no clear strategy for how I could afford to support this increase in demand. So I went to the New York Small Business Development Center, a free resource, where I was actually told, "You are a Black woman, there must be tons of free grant money out there for you." This was not the first time that someone had said this to me. I had heard rumors of government grants and corporate initiatives to support Black and brown entrepreneurs. But actually finding those resources was another thing entirely.

I had, however, applied for the Council of Fashion Designers of America (CFDA) Eco-Fashion Challenge, which was essentially a grant for fashion businesses that adhered to a sustainable model for all or parts of their collection. I was not even sure how they were defining "sustainable" but thought Brother Vellies was a great fit. Plus, the prize money was seventy-five thousand dollars, a staggering amount for someone like me. But first, I needed a detailed business plan with financial projections to be eligible.

At the New York Small Business Development Center, I was introduced to Ricardo, an African American man my age with a gentle voice and a disarming smile. I showed him everything I had and told him that I felt way in over my head. I explained that the financial wherewithal of running this business on a shoestring budget was overwhelming, and that I thought often of all the artisans, how excited they were to be part of this company and how much they were counting on me to get it right. That was when I began to cry.

"No need to get emotional," he said kindly. "We can figure this out." He patiently explained the process and then worked with me to map out the projections, ensuring I understood all of it.

"Don't worry," he assured me. "They don't even teach people how to do tax returns in school and those are required annually by every person living in this country! It's nothing to be ashamed of to not know how to run projections or make high-level business plans for your company. If you didn't grow up in a family like that or have the resources to secure an MBA, how would you know?"

At that point, I was taking every single dollar I made and spending it on the business. I was also doing everything myself, from the packing and shipping to handwriting the labels. I responded to every customer service call or email, as well. My business strategy was simply to keep as many shoes in stock as possible, sell them, and use that money to buy more shoes.

I also offered pre-orders for shoes, so that I would have the funds to make them. But the issue was always that I never had enough shoes to meet the demand. The thought of finding an investor, or raising capital, never crossed my mind. It just wasn't in my realm of possibility. At the time, I was not close with anyone who had done that and these were never topics at my dinner table growing up.

On my next trip to Kenya, I sat down with Makeda to create something new that honored how the Maasai traditionally wore beading. Makeda had been making beaded sandals for more than a decade for locals and tourists, so the capability was there. What I went on to call the Maasai sandal was a classic strappy sandal that wrapped up the calf to the knee, gladiator-like, with a beaded front panel along the length of the shin. I wanted the women in the workshop to create their own intricate patterns for those pieces, and Makeda was as excited as I was to let them be creative.

The samples we made on that trip were exquisite. Like muk-luks, each shoe was an opportunity for these women to take artistic license and tell their own stories. Before I returned to Brooklyn, Makeda suggested that we allow some of the local women to do the beading work at home.

"This will give mothers with no access to childcare the abil-ity to earn a living," she explained.

"Absolutely!" I said. My heart felt full knowing that the po-tential success of this shoe might help dozens of moms.

On October 8, 2014, I posted a sketch of the Maasai sandal on my Instagram account. The next day, Vogue.com featured a pair made in the workshop using the bone beads I had sourced in Kibera from the man in the market. Another Brother Vellies shoe had officially launched.

Meanwhile, I was scrambling to fulfill all the orders that were coming in. Olivia Kim at Nordstrom had made a huge order of Tyre sandals. She also gave me eight display windows at the main entrances of the busiest Nordstrom locations, prime real estate usually reserved for famous designers. This was a major vote of confidence for Brother Vellies, and the best kind of brand awareness.

Then Makeda called me, panicked. "We have a problem," she said. "Our shipment was stolen."

"What?" I said.

"The Tyre sandals were taken," she said. Her voice was shaky. "By al-Shabab."

"Are you telling me that a terrorist organization has our sandals?"

"Yes."

I had to take a beat to process this.

"What are we going to do?" I asked.

"They want money," she said.

"Makeda!" I cried into the phone.

"I had to tell you because I was worried," she said.

The next few days played out as slow as molasses until I was awoken by a phone call. It was Makeda. "We got them back," she said, palpably relieved. I let out a big sigh.

"How?" I asked.

"Oh boy!" she said, laughing, and I felt immediately relieved.

In those days in between, I had been worried sick. I felt completely helpless. But I knew better than to ask for details. This was her community, her business, and her relationships—

I was just relieved that everyone was okay and that we were back on track.

But then, the same thing happened with the next shipment.

I was worried about Makeda, and the safety of all the women who worked with her. I also could not afford to deliver late—we had started to get a lot of press and delivering late to retailers was the kiss of death. If your order delivery deadline is not met, the retailer has the right to cancel it, meaning all the money you spent on that product is lost—and you no longer have a buyer. Brother Vellies had no savings or bank credit to weather that kind of financial blow. So when the second shipment was stolen, I did not know where to turn. One particularly desperate afternoon, I started googling "international fashion emergency" and "the United Nations." That was how the Ethical Fashion Initiative of the United Nations popped up. I immediately sent an email to the "info" address listed on the site explaining the situation.

Sending that cold email felt like tossing a message in a bottle into a big blue ocean, so I was over the moon to receive a response: "Thank you for getting in touch with us, Aurora!"

Simone Cipriani, creator of the Ethical Fashion Initiative, which is a joint program between the U.N. and the International Trade Centre, responded by asking to meet with me. I couldn't believe my luck.

His email included a questionnaire about my business: Where were the workshops? Who was working with me? Did I have look books? Where was I selling the product?

I was typing so fast to answer him, my fingers clicking as quickly as my heart was beating.

His next email suggested we meet the following day, at a Starbucks in Times Square. It turned out he happened to be in town. The stars were aligning. When I entered the bustling coffee shop, I spotted him, an older Italian man with salt-and-pepper hair and a matching bushy beard. He was dressed impeccably in a navy blue Cucinelli wool suit.

"You must be Aurora," he said in a thick, rolling Italian accent, with a big warm smile and outstretched arms. I knew from the moment we met that I could trust him and that he would be able to help me. He told me that he had been following our press and that he believed Brother Vellies had a huge potential to reshape the idea of value creation within the global artisan landscape.

"Aurora, what you are doing is exceptional," he said, his eyes twinkling. "I see all the ways that it could lead to more employment opportunities for artisans with Brother Vellies, and also beyond!"

He was the first person I'd met, beyond the artisans themselves, who I knew truly understood what we were doing, and how impactful it could be. I grew emotional, standing there at the bar, sipping espresso as early-morning commuters scurried in and out of the coffee shop on their way to work.

"I looked at everything you sent, and we are going to help you," he said with a big smile.

He went on to describe the U.N.'s support programs, and how Brother Vellies met all the criteria. I had never been told that I met the criteria for anything. I didn't even have a credit score. In a world where I felt like I was constantly skating by, it was so gratifying to have someone telling me the work I was doing had value far and above the scorecards I had been measuring myself against. There were so many things that I wanted to do for the company and for the artisans, and we were always falling just a little bit short. I didn't realize it then, but it was statistically a miracle that I was even still in business at this point.

He told me that they wanted to run an impact assessment of Brother Vellies, looking at the margins, the conditions of the workshops, and to help find other workshops that could benefit from the employment opportunities Brother Vellies was creating. I had fallen in love with the process of designing shoes but was also heavily restricted by our workshops' capacities. Technologically speaking, we were forty years and forty million dollars behind our competitors.

Then he asked me, "What is your dream?"

"To be able to create a high heel that can empower women instead of holding them back," I said.

He held up his paper cup to clink with mine.

"A worthy goal!" he said. "Andiamo!"

On October 29, 2014, I learned that a jewelry brand called K/LLER COLLECTION had won the CFDA Eco-Fashion Challenge: I'd thought I had a good chance of winning that award, and the seventy-five thousand dollars in prize money that came with it, so this was hard news. My company mission was based on sustainability in a variety of ways—not just the materials used, but the communities impacted. I asked for constructive feedback and learned that Brother Vellies was causing concern for allowing the women to do the beadwork from home on the Maasai sandals.

I was shocked. I had considered that a great solution for childcare, one of the most challenging issues for working mothers, but one of the judges felt it was unsafe.

"Why?" I asked, utterly confused.

"Well, she could be forcing her children to do the labor!" was the judge's answer. This was a textbook example of an American thinking she knew what was best for Africa without ever having visited the continent, let alone the specific place where these shoes were made. My dreams of using that prize money to help purchase new equipment for the workshops, or hire a new employee, were dashed.

I still had no access to capital and my DHL shipping bills were exorbitant. All I could do was stay focused on our mission and continue to grow my business and strengthen my relationships with both the artisans and the retailers. Our rental arrangement at South Street Seaport helped make it possible: Some months, rent was sixty-five dollars. Others, it was fifteen hundred. Only having to pay a set percentage of sales allowed me to stay afloat even in the slow months. The press remained favorable, and I started to get asked more about "luxury" as it pertained to Africa. That led to an invitation to speak at Harvard University as part of "A Conversation About Luxury Goods."

There was no greater example of this than our Maasai sandal, which was why that judge's comments were so disheartening. They were part of our spring collection that year and special because no two were alike. They were costly given how long they took to bead, adorned with ostrich feathers, which were mailed in from South Africa and had been hand-dyed one by one. I was worried they would be too expensive for our tiny company to sell. At the time, we were selling Vellies for $235, which some people complained was too expensive. I received emails saying they should be cheaper because they were made in Africa and emails asking if my website was a Nigerian scam. The barrage of microaggressions was exhausting. So, when the editor of *Vogue France* asked me how much the Maasai sandals were, I said with confidence, "Twelve hundred dollars." I wanted to prove my thesis: These shoes deserved to be as much as or more than Valentino.

Sophia Amoruso and I had met a couple of times by then during my time in L.A. Nasty Gal had reached out in the past to see if they could sell Brother Vellies. As a company, I wanted to focus on the luxury sector, and I saw that Nasty Gal was quickly devolving into a fast-fashion site. I looked up to her as a strong female entrepreneur. She was innovative and brilliant, but in a lot of ways, her story and journey scared me because for all the celebrations of her success, it felt like the company was losing its identity. For that reason, my answer was always no.

Until I had a proposition. I called the buyer at Nasty Gal and said, "I can offer you fifty pairs of our Maasai sandals."

I knew that would provide an income for the Maasai women we were working with at that time, as well as pay for our upcoming collection. I needed to pay my artisans up front, versus the more traditional factory arrangements, where you can pay after delivery. Nasty Gal agreed. This meant Makeda could commission another fifty pairs; up until that point, we had only made ten.

That same week, *Vogue Paris* anointed it the shoe of the week. American *Vogue* ran a story on our artisan work, and we had a full page in *Elle Canada*. The best part for me was sending all the magazines featuring the sandals to Makeda to share with the women who made them. I wanted them to see that their work was just as worthy as any glossy European designer's. And they were so proud. Makeda pinned every image to the workshop walls, so everyone could see. I also sent them copies of Sophia's book, *#Girlboss*.

I felt the CFDA Eco-Fashion Challenge judges missed the point and rather than letting that deter me, I decided to lean in and apply for the CFDA's Fashion Incubator program. It is a two-year program for emerging designers that, in June 2015, came with office space and a mentorship for designers. I also applied to the CFDA/Vogue Fashion Fund, which was created in the wake of 9/11 by Anna Wintour and the CFDA to support emerging designers following the economic crash caused by the terrorist attacks. For that coveted award, ten designers are selected to compete, and the prize is a combination of money for your business and mentorship, as well as press in *Vogue*. I knew it was a long shot, but I also had nothing to lose. It was every designer's dream—and often a lifeline; the award money was three hundred thousand dollars. At the very least, I knew it was a chance to have my work viewed by the judges: That year they were Diane von Furstenberg; Jenna Lyons, the creative director of J.Crew; Ken Downing from Neiman Marcus; Steven Kolb, the president of the CFDA; Mark Holgate, a senior editor at *Vogue;* Anna Wintour; investor Andrew Rosen; Eva Chen, the fashion director from Instagram; and Jeffrey Kalinsky of Jeffrey, the luxury department store. Just getting my brand seen by them in the application process was worth it to me. I viewed this as an incredible access opportunity in an industry that was so historically closed-door. And applying was free.

Only sixty people were given formal applications, so I was thrilled when I got the email that invited me to the next level. For that, I answered a wide range of questions: What are your dreams for your line? Where is it made? What is the ethos behind your brand? Which department stores do you sell to? And which publications have featured your work?

I didn't tell any of my friends that I was applying because my business was still so young, and I was full of self-doubt. The application asked a lot of questions about both you and your brand. I answered the one about my "formal" training honestly: Everything I know about designing and creating shoes, I learned on the ground in workshops in Africa. I was not Parsons-trained, nor had I done an internship with Manolo Blahnik. Makeda and John were my mentors.

I was in Morocco for a production trip when I received an email saying I had made it to the second round. I was now among thirty designers competing for ten spots. I could not believe this was happening. Now I had to submit a video explaining why being in the Fashion Fund was important to me and my brand. I decided to do it right there, in Marrakesh. Jason set up his iPhone on a pile of books doubling as a makeshift tripod and shot me sitting in a rattan chair in the mosaic tiled courtyard of the hotel where we were staying. In the video, I am surrounded by vibrant leaves, with parakeets and magpies singing in the background. It was very low-tech, but it also felt very right as I happened to be there working on the latest babouche and new carved wooden clogs for Brother Vellies. I knew that sustainability had "crunchy" Bohemian connotations that working with artisans in Africa further fueled. I also knew that most fashion designers did not look like me.

I spoke from my heart about how and why I started Brother Vellies with the goal of working with craftsmen and craftswomen all throughout Africa, explaining in a shaky, high-pitched voice that "I use a lot of traditional African techniques in my designing, like bone carving and indigo dyeing. A lot of the shapes are rooted in traditional African shoe shapes, like the Moroccan babouche and the South African Vellie." I ended by saying how I felt I was ready to be in the Fashion Fund and how I believed it would take my business to the next level.

I also had to submit a formal application in the form of a book that told the story behind the brand. This was a much bigger undertaking. I had heard so many urban legends about the process. My friend Anja worked at the Launch Collective and told me that Pamela Love's application was an elaborate three-by-two-foot jewelry box made of wood that had a twirling ballerina version of herself inside and six wooden drawers, each containing a sample of her jewelry. There was another famous rumored story about a designer who put his application on a CD-ROM and delivered it in a ziplock bag with his name scribbled across it in Sharpie. Other designers' applications were apparently so elaborate that they went on to be acquired by the Metropolitan Museum of Art.

Back in New York, I found a bookmaker in midtown Manhattan who typically focused on hand-binding Bibles. I brought him a springbok hide from South Africa that we meticulously used together to bind a cover. I called my friend Kyle Hagler, a beloved agent known for representing African American models whom I had worked with during my time assisting Jennifer Starr. I asked if he would tell Grace Mahary, an Eritrean Canadian model, about Brother Vellies and the mission, as she seemed the exact right fit for our first campaign. I knew she cared deeply about elevating Africa in the fashion world. I was thrilled when Kyle told me she had agreed to do the shoot in exchange for a pair of the Maasai sandals.

Jason shot all the images for the book, including one of me having breakfast with a giraffe that he took in Kenya. Below that, I wrote about my first trip to Africa. *This mesmerizing continent I had only dreamt about suddenly came to life before me. I fell in love with Namibia's never-ending skies and Morocco's hypnotic winding souks. But it was the people and the artisans I fell in love with the most. After years of wanting to realize my dreams as a designer, it was through them that both of our dreams became possible.* I signed it, as I still do today and have since kindergarten, making the A in Aurora in the shape of a heart.

The pages that followed were filled with images taken in both Africa and Brooklyn. A photo of me in the Kenyan workshop alongside Makeda, and another shot of the first pair of babouche made from reclaimed denim. The hand-carved bone beads alongside a version of the Maasai sandal that incorporated them, as well as images of an assortment of shoes that I had made to date: simple slides, springbok sandals, Tyre sandals, and various Vellies for kids.

I also made a motorcycle jacket out of springbok, which I

added alongside my own mood board: a Joan Didion quote; a 1966 photo of Donyale Luna, the first Black supermodel; and some Technicolor flowers. I selected several versions of the Tyre sandals, all made from different leathers and furs, including rabbit sourced from a multi-generational farm in Kenya. And four different types of Vellies using Mickalene Thomas's textiles from a collaboration we had done. One of the questions was, "Which celebrities have worn your product?" so I taped the Maasai sandals onto Beyoncé, and then set an intention: One day she would.

One of my favorite photos is of Grace wearing my grandmother's fur, the Werther's butterscotch still in the pocket.

I placed this seventy-five-page book, the Brother Vellies story, in a wooden box with a stained-glass version of our logo that reminded me of my mom. The box was lined with mirrors, so whoever opened it would see themselves in that space. I put my whole heart into that application, centering the artisans, their work, their artistry. I knew that since I had made it to this second round, the judges would review my work and learn about Brother Vellies. That already felt like a dream come true.

I was at home in Bed-Stuy on a Tuesday morning when the doorbell rang. I opened the door to a film crew, but before I could ask what on earth they were doing, my phone rang in my hand: It was Steven Kolb, the head of the CFDA.

"Congratulations, Aurora!" he said. "You made it to the final ten!"

A feeling I had never experienced before washed over me. It

felt like every single moment of hard work had paid off. I was being given an extraordinary opportunity and so was everyone else who made Brother Vellies possible.

"As for the film crew . . ." He went on to explain that the CFDA was doing a non-scripted television show of the Fashion Fund process for Amazon Prime Video. I was elated! It made sense to be part of *this* reality TV show.

Being accepted into the Fashion Fund meant the opportunity to have ten of the most influential people in the fashion industry focus on our brand. After I hung up with Steven and the film crew left, I called Makeda to share the news.

"We got into the Fashion Fund!" I shouted, delirious, into the phone, tears streaming down my face.

"Oh my God, this is a blessing!" she screamed back. "But also, what is this?"

"A very big deal!" I squealed into the phone. "Plus, we are going to be on TV!"

"You are making us famous!" Makeda laughed with full-throated glee. "I cannot wait to tell the others!"

Anna Wintour presided over our very first meeting. I was in the room with Scott Studenberg and John Targon of Baja East; Matt Baldwin of Baldwin Denim and Co.; Cadet's Brad Schmidt and Raul Arevalo; Chris Gelinas of CG; Becca McCharen of Chromat; Gypsy Sport's Rio Uribe; as well as Jonathan Simkhai, Thaddeus O'Neil, and David Hart, who each had their own namesake label. My mindset was collaboration over competition. I hoped to strike up friendships with all of them. I was sticking to the idea that when creative people support one another, we all rise together.

After introductions were made, Anna informed us that the competition would be based on our spring 2016 collections, which we would show at New York Fashion Week that September. She added that the film crew would follow us throughout the process, including the moment the winner was announced, at a gala in November. That was when we also learned that the prize money that year was not three hundred thousand dollars, but four hundred thousand!

"You have six weeks to pull it all together," Anna said coolly, sunglasses on.

I might have let out an audible sigh of relief; as the only accessories designer, I thought I was off the hook, as usually only clothing designers stage fashion shows where people come to watch models parade down the runway. People like me who make shoes and bags usually invite editors and buyers to come to their showroom for private, low-key appointments.

But then, as if she had read my mind, Anna looked at me and purred, "Even you, Aurora."

For a moment, I wondered if I had bitten off more than I could chew. I had five dollars in my bank account, literally. How on earth could I pull off a runway show? I still had a company to run, and orders to fill. I knew this would ultimately be great for my business, but it would take resources I did not have. So I channeled everything I learned at Gen Art.

My friend Dana was helping with my PR at the time, and we sent a few feeler emails to potential brand partners to see who might be interested in sponsoring my show. I was thrilled when Sephora enthusiastically responded—a woman named Blakeley Vaugh was senior director of external communications at the beauty retailer—and they offered to send a full glam team for the models and sponsor us to the tune of ten thousand dollars. Phew! I had a budget—albeit small—for my first ever show.

Next, I needed models, and so I wrote to every agent I knew and then tweeted an L.A.-based model and friend named Adesuwa to ask if she was coming to New York anytime soon.

She replied, "Should I?"

I said, "Yes!" She was excited to be participating in her first New York Fashion Week. She became my fit model and later went on to grace the cover of *Vogue* many times.

As all of us scrambled to pull together our collections, we were simultaneously being scheduled to meet with the judges to present early ideas. All ten of the judges were set to come at different times to meet me at my store. To be honest, I was a little bit nervous to have them come by. I loved the store but did not have the budget a lot of designers did. Still, it was beautiful. I had hand-painted the walls using a checkered diamond pattern reminiscent of South Africa. We had stacked milk crates and topped them with mattress foam to create seating. And Makeda had sent us a hundred meters of fringed raffia, which we used on some of the back walls and made it feel like Kenya was coming alive in the space. Pictures of our artisans were hung throughout the store, and each pair of shoes sat, laces perfectly tied and feathers perfectly fluffed, on its own pedestal in the space.

Jenna Lyons was the first to visit. She told me that I always need to have things that retailed for less than fifty dollars at the cash register. She suggested socks. Every time I would see her, she'd say, "Did you launch socks yet?" (She was right about those.) Diane von Furstenberg came into the space with shopping on her mind. After bringing a half dozen shoes to the register, she asked, "Where are the handbags?" She said that it would be silly of me to not translate my aesthetic sensibility into handbags. Ken Downing came in and announced that he loved coming down to the Seaport. Andrew Rosen arrived and said that he hated coming down to the Seaport. He also suggested that I stick to Vellies. Mark Holgate came in, all smiles as always. He was consistently the person who made me feel the most accepted, no matter where we were or what I was doing. Anna was immediately fascinated, picking up everything and going straight to the mood board, wanting to get a clear understanding of what my inspiration was and what made me tick. Steven Kolb came in and loved the space and the unique point of view he thought I was bringing to the tapestry and the New York designer landscape. He made it known that the line of communication was always open.

I was proud to be in a cohort with these designers, but quickly realized many of them had more resources and connections than I did. At one point, we were flown to Los Angeles and put up at the Sunset Tower Hotel. There, the judges announced a surprise Instagram challenge—the app was just launching video—so we were tasked with shooting a promotional video on our iPhones in a historic L.A. landmark that was on-brand.

After they announced this challenge, I was slumped on the couch next to Jonathan Simkhai, who designed classic pretty dresses in flattering shapes. He turned to me with a broad smile and whispered, "I already have a full film crew, director, and a drone camera booked." The wind left my sails. Jonathan's brother had created Grindr, so he was a pro at all things tech and social—his business had launched with capital. And apparently he had enough intel to find out about challenges before they were even announced.

I thought, "How on earth am I supposed to compete with this?"

When I first arrived in the United States, Fresh and I would hike up to the Hollywood Sign to eat sandwiches out of brown paper bags and drink Snapple and talk about our dreams. I decided to film something up there myself. I hiked up to that iconic sign and then read a passage from Jack Kerouac's *On the Road,* which echoed some of the struggles I had been going through. As I looked out at the same vista with a new perspective, it reaffirmed what a long way I had come, and how I was on the right path.

Eva Chen, who was Instagram's fashion director and judging this particular challenge, said that she loved the film: She told me that it felt raw and authentic. It was certainly a part of my journey that I had not shared. I was spending so much time trying to keep it together, appear organized, and project the idea of luxury—albeit with a touch of my mom's Boho aesthetic. It dawned on me that a lot of people were forming incorrect assumptions about me and where I came from. So I decided to just be myself.

Constantly being filmed added an extra layer of intensity to the entire endeavor, and every decision felt high stakes. Since I had not gone to Parsons, or Central Saint Martins, I had to rely on the one thing that was entirely mine: my instincts.

And every once in a while, when I was feeling down or over-whelmed, an encouraging note from Anna would magically appear in my email.

Meanwhile, everyone in the workshops in Kenya, Morocco, and South Africa was turbocharged. We did the traditional Moroccan babouche made from discarded denim that had been piling up just outside of Marrakesh. We did the Maasai sandal, the Tyre sandal, and a new shoe I designed called the Dhara sandal. I used an old fur coat that I cut up to add pieces on the front of the sandal. I also used dyed chicken feathers that I initially sourced from farms in Africa to adorn another sandal called the Lamu, and created the Burkina sandal, a slide that utilized fabric hand-woven in Burkina Faso, one of the new workshops Simone found for me.

I was so proud of the collection. There had been so many other designers who had utilized African prints before, but rarely were they printed or woven in Africa. Many high-end shoe designers had used beadwork before, but as far as I know, it'd never been beaded in Africa. I felt proud to be a shepherd of all these amazingly talented artisans, most of whom were multi-generational in their craft. I just hoped and prayed that the judges would get it.

It was late August and we were full steam ahead prepping for the September show, when a friend texted me to ask for the details. "Can you send the address and date?" he wrote. "Kanye West wants to come."

"Ok!" I wrote back hastily, sending the address. I was too busy to ask any follow-up questions.

The next week, my assistant called me in a panic: The Nasty Gal buyer had called her to claim that bugs had been detected in the Maasai sandals they had ordered. She wanted to return all fifty pairs and was demanding a full refund. I was dumbfounded. I called Makeda, heartbroken and embarrassed at even having to ask her what the chances were that bugs had made their way onto our shoes.

"That is not possible," she said stonily, understandably upset. "There are no bugs in our work!"

I believed her. It did not make sense: We had exported them through the correct channels, which included a routine export fumigation. Still, the buyer at Nasty Gal wanted the $25,000 payment for the shoes reimbursed. But I did not have it to give her. At that point, our entire revenue was $150,000. I was certain that the bugs were not from the shoes. But I did wonder, "Could it be the boxes?"

We had commissioned woven baskets, also made in Kenya, to replace a traditional cardboard box. We'd put a ton of effort into them, and it had paid off: They were beautiful.

I was on the phone with the buyer when I asked, "Where do you think they got the bugs?" I was still trying to figure it out myself.

"Aren't the women sitting on dirt floors when they are making these shoes?" she said in an accusatory tone. Clearly, her only understanding of Africa had been formed through watching World Vision and UNICEF commercials.

I caught my breath before I responded. "No, they do not sit on dirt floors."

"Then they must have gotten them on the boat," she countered. I could feel her contempt through the phone.

"These shoes were never on a boat," I said. "They were flown here. On Delta."

This woman, who was high up at Nasty Gal, was ruthless.

"If this gets out, this is going to ruin your chances at winning the Fashion Fund," she said. "And you certainly don't want me to tell Sophia."

The buyer did not know that I had a relationship with Sophia, and I was certain that she would have disapproved of the woman speaking to me or about us in this way. And while I debated calling Sophia myself, I was truly too humiliated and scared. I just wanted to figure this out.

I had to find out if the shoes did indeed arrive with bugs. Or if we were being blamed for something that was not our fault. Either way, I did not have the money to reimburse them $25,000. And I certainly did not want word to get out that Brother Vellies' shoes were infested. This kind of press could indeed derail our chances of winning the Fashion Fund—and ruin my fledgling business.

I decided to go to the fulfillment center in Kentucky with Samantha the very next day to see the so-called bugs. This was tricky as I was in the middle of shooting for the Amazon show and had to do it secretively. My lawyer told me to take videos and pictures and had made special arrangements to have a bug specialist on standby. We arrived at the warehouse wearing blue latex gloves. Samantha had fashioned herself an elaborate hazmat suit. We were not the women for the job, but nonetheless, there we were. I thought it was possible that the bugs might have come from the dry-grass boxes, so we examined every pair of shoes and its box. I opened each box slowly and deliberately. I even came with a magnifying glass to investigate, and plastic specimen bags to collect samples.

With every box I opened, I was able to breathe more easily: We found nothing.

Then, on box 44 of 50, we found two tiny bugs on one shoe, each roughly the size of a pinhead. I snapped a photo and sent it to my lawyer. Within minutes, he texted me back: "Bedbugs." He added, "It is not possible that they came in from Kenya."

Bedbugs, he explained, are commonly found in America. The expert said it was impossible for the bugs to survive the fumigation the shoes had before they left Kenya, but also that their life span was such that they could not have been born there and still be alive today. Too much time had passed.

I turned to the women working at the warehouse who were helping us, feeling both relieved and outraged: "Have you ever had any bedbug issues in the warehouse?" I asked casually.

"We get them in here all the time," she responded.

I waited until I was back in New York to call the buyer from Nasty Gal.

In the end, the shoes were taken down from the website. We quarantined the pairs we already had in NYC in a giant industrial freezer to be safe, even though we were certain they were already bug-free. Eventually, we sold a handful on special request and archived the remaining pairs. Customers who paid the full price for those shoes loved them, and whenever someone bought a pair, it made my whole week.

While a public crisis was averted, I was still heartbroken. So many of these beautiful shoes just disappeared. Each was made with love and pride by these incredible women in Kenya—they deserved to be celebrated. I also learned that there were going to be situations, even with people who said they wanted to support the brand, where unconscious biases might impact the relationship and business. Retailers are a very specific beast.

People are quick to tell you who they are, what they care about. But they don't always know how to live the values they espouse. They don't know what the ideology looks like from an implementation standpoint. You can say you want to support goods that are handmade on the continent of Africa. But if you are unable to wait a little bit longer for these goods, or spend a little bit more so the workers can be paid a living wage, then what does your support mean? You have to ask yourself if the way you live your life is in unison with the implementation of the values you claim to hold.

Just because you buy one "good" thing today does not negate the damage of bad things you have bought in the past.

Just because you buy carbon offsets for your footprint today does not mean that you have neutralized the damage your business has already done to society.

Just because you want to be better now doesn't mean you were not bad before. Old habits die hard.

14

Winning isn't everything

Crisis averted, I returned to New York in mid-August to prepare for my first Brother Vellies show during fashion week in September. I was happy with the shoes I had designed but was having a difficult time casting enough Black models to participate. Every time I called an agency to ask for a specific model, I learned that they were tied up in exclusives with bigger brands. In a panic, I cold-called Bethann Hardison, a former model and agent who worked as an activist for inclusivity in the fashion world. She explained to me that what I was experiencing was par for the course. The agents felt like the only way a Black model could break into the scene was by debuting with a huge brand, like Celine. So when a casting director took a liking to any of the models of color, they were put on exclusive—which meant they could not work for anyone else.

I was confused.

"Have you ever heard of a house nigger?" Bethann asked bluntly.

That was a punch in the stomach and added a new layer of complexity.

In the end, I was able to piece together a handful of Black models who were available and asked my friend Adesuwa, who had flown in from L.A., to stay for the show. She agreed and wound up front and center in my presentation.

The day of the show, the male and female models sat on a collection of vintage chairs placed on pedestals in a loft-like room, so people could really see their shoes, which had been made in Kenya, South Africa, Ethiopia, and Morocco. I loved each pair: gender-neutral Vellies in a bold checkers print, color-ful carved clogs, and sandals of all varieties adorned in feathers or beadwork. There was no glitz or glam or crazy front row at my show. It was my little offering, and I was so proud of it. Kanye wound up coming, and sang our praises, which meant added press in addition to the already glowing reviews of the collection. I was relieved to pull it off, especially with such little money. Most of the models did it in exchange for shoes and told me they felt proud to be a part of something that felt so special and different. I was grateful and spent the majority of the pre-sentation in tears.

Following the September shows, *Vogue* hosted a dinner in L.A., which was also filmed. I was talking to someone when Anna Wintour arrived wearing one of Jonathan Simkhai's gor-geous floral dresses. My heart dropped: It had never occurred to me to send Anna a pair of shoes. It was such a missed opportunity. I was so disappointed in myself and ended up drinking too much that evening.

At one point, one of the producers pulled me into the greenroom to do an interview. By then, I was so drunk that I had completely forgotten we were being filmed.

"Who do you think is going to win?" the producer asked as the cameras rolled.

"Duh. Isn't it obvious?" I said, rolling my eyes. "*Simkhai.*" The camera crew loved me because I was never strategic and always honest, especially that night. I eventually found out that there were memes of me crying in every episode of the Fashion Fund show.

The designers John and Scott from Baja East were also frontrunners to win. Both were very good-looking. One worked for Lanvin and the other let it be known that he was friends with Marc Jacobs. They had already received several credits in *Vogue*. I felt I was clearly out of my league. The other designers had either worked at fashion houses or had gone to design school. Meanwhile, I'd learned everything I knew about making shoes in workshops in Namibia, South Africa, and Kenya. While that was precisely the point of Brother Vellies, I was definitely a stand-alone amongst this group of emerging talent. I stayed super positive, but definitely suffered from crippling imposter syndrome.

Getting accepted into the Fashion Fund also meant a fullpage photo shoot with *Vogue,* where each designer was paired with a model and a musician. I thought Solange would be a great fit but then Selby Drummond, the accessories director at *Vogue* and main designer liaison for the program, called me to ask how I felt about A$AP Rocky as my musical match.

To begin with, I did not consider being paired with just any celebrity a win—especially not a male rapper who had no relationship with the brand or the values that I was trying to establish.

"Not great," I said. "But if it has to be him, then I am going to be standing on him in the photo."

Selby laughed. "That's a great answer," she said.

However, they switched out A$AP for two other musicians: Shamir and Grimes. Shamir wrote thoughtful songs and dressed in a way that obscured his gender, and Grimes was a thoughtful, independent, feminist musician. That made more sense to me. She also showed up late and had not shaved her legs, much to the dismay of the editor. I did not mind at all; she reminded me of my mom. But she did wind up getting dropped from the photo, leaving me, Shamir, and Kendall Jenner. Kendall was an up-and-coming model at the time, who had come over to my apartment in Bed-Stuy with her mom a year earlier to do a test shoot with Jason when she first signed with her modeling agent, Ashleah. She was supersweet and young and excited to be kicking off her career. Because of our history, she also made sense to me, and Brother Vellies. She wore the Maasai sandals and a beaded Rodarte dress. The hairdresser decided to plait her hair into two long, messy fishtail braids.

When I look back at that photo now, it feels a little like indigenous appropriation. And while one of the creatives directing the shoot was indigenous, when you see the photo, if it lacks context, it begs the questions: Who gets to reference different cultures? Who gets to wear a Maasai sandal? Who gets to wear beading? I did not have the answers—then or now—but these felt like important questions to be asking, especially as I continued on with this brand.

The idea of cultural appropriation versus celebration was and is slippery and shape-shifting. Then, people were starting to realize it was offensive to wear a feathered headdress to Coachella or dress up in blackface at Halloween. Before, this had been common practice in many spaces. I started wondering what that meant for certain elements of African craftsmanship that we were utilizing at Brother Vellies. I had these conversations constantly with the artisans, and their general take was that it made them excited when they saw their designs on people. Putting traditional African skill sets into a luxury equation was validating for them. So we agreed that *we* wanted everyone in the world to be able to wear Brother Vellies.

At the awards ceremony Zendaya was my official "date." Anna paired us, as she often did for designers. Although I did not own a TV and had no idea who Zendaya was at the time, I was happy that she had agreed. My research told me that she was this young, smart, and super-talented actress who also seemed incredibly down-to-earth—traits that inspired me. Her stylist, Law Roach, introduced himself to me at one of the first CFDA/Vogue Fashion Fund events and I immediately liked his vibrancy, the way he saw the world, and his deep appreciation of fashion as an art form.

It was a buzzy and exciting evening, with a room full of familiar faces—Tom Ford, Prabal Gurung, the women from

Cushnie et Ochs, Diane von Furstenberg, Jenna Lyons, Chioma from *Vogue,* and Christian Louboutin. Andra Day performed "Rise Up," which was so moving I obviously cried.

The time finally came to announce the winner, and we all took our seats as Riccardo Tisci, Givenchy's creative director at that time, walked up to the podium with Amanda Seyfried. I wanted Becca from Chromat to win. She was the only other woman competing and her dedication to dressing diverse body types was authentic. She was counterculture in a way that felt new for *Vogue,* and I appreciated the way they leaned into her. Her designs were innovative, and the judges really liked her. She and I had become fast friends.

Then Riccardo announced with a sly smile, "For the first time in the history of the CFDA/Vogue Fashion Fund, we have a three-way tie!"

The audience gasped. My stomach dropped. Then Amanda opened the envelope and began to read names from the card: "Aurora James of Brother Vellies, Jonathan Simkhai, and Rio Uribe of Gypsy Sport."

I was in so much shock that the thunderous applause grew more distant, as if I was being pulled away from it, floating. In that moment, my mind was flooded with all the people that I had worked with along the way who had helped me get to this moment. Makeda, and her broad smile; the Nguni farmer who sold me that first pelt; John, showing me around the workshop when we met; the bone carver from the Nairobi market; my babouche vendor from Marrakesh. I was winning this award on behalf of their artistry and work, which had never been cele-brated in this way. As I gathered myself to walk up onto the stage, I knew that I wanted to make this point: I was not winning this award. We were.

I stepped onto the stage, entirely unsure of what to say. I had nothing prepared, and yet the words started tumbling out of my mouth: "Everything I have learned about shoemaking, I learned across tiny workshops in Africa."

I asked the room, including some of the most successful designers in the world, to think about how they could take Black bodies off their mood boards and put them onto their payrolls and include them in the financial proposition of whatever they were making and selling.

"Instead of just taking inspiration from these people," I said, "think about how you could involve them in your actual process." I received a standing ovation. That night, whether it was true or not, I felt like everyone in that room had become my family.

The next day, I called my mother to share the news.

"Aurora, that's wonderful, but when are you going to stop competing in systems that were not made for you?" was all she said.

15

target on my back

The first thing I did with the prize money was hire a more senior staff member in January 2016. I knew I needed another team member to help me grow Brother Vellies, someone with experience. Around that same time, I had also been accepted into the CFDA Fashion Incubator program, which started in May 2016. Typically, designers do the Incubator before even applying to the Fashion Fund, but the timing felt prescient. Brother Vellies was getting attention, and I wanted to scale into more retail stores and grow the brand. I knew the bigger we got, the more impact we could have.

At the Incubator I was one of ten brands (twelve designers), including Thaddeus O'Neil, who had been with me in the Fashion Fund, and Alexandra Alvarez from the brand Alix. The purpose of the Incubator was to form community and share information, networks, and resources. It also came with office space on Thirty-eighth Street in a building that was full of other successful designers. It was built as a two-year program that functioned as a fashion accelerator, which was aimed at helping burgeoning young designers take their business to the next level.

Target was billed as the major sponsor, but oddly, we were still expected to pay rent for the office space. That led to Kerby from Pyer Moss dropping out early on. Most of us could barely afford it, and I did not understand why we were paying anything if it was sponsored by a corporation like Target. Ironically, even though I had co-won the fund and got a huge amount of money, I still couldn't afford to move out of my Bed-Stuy apartment. I had been with Jason for six years by then, but could not balance work and my personal life. I was also in a reality TV show, filmed partially in our home, as our relationship was breaking down. We decided to split up, which was really hard on both of us. Even harder was that we lived together for another year because I could not afford to leave: All of the money had to be funneled into Brother Vellies.

Then one day, Rick Gomez, the chief marketing officer of Target, came to speak with the Incubator designers.

"Every designer wants to do a collaboration with Target," he announced with a big smile.

"Not me," I thought, irritated by the assumption.

He went on to do a presentation about what a happy place Target was, and how everyone loved the company. I was feeling

increasingly uncomfortable the more he spoke because I did not
agree with anything that he was saying. The final straw was
when he said, "Target is the most beloved place in the world
other than Disneyland!" I heard my mother's voice in my head:
"If someone has to tell you that they are great, then that is probably not true." This prompted me to speak up.

"That is fascinating," I said. "Because I got very different
feedback from my audience."

I shared the experience I'd had a year earlier when I went to
Target on Atlantic Avenue in Brooklyn to buy a razor. I wanted
a black, or a beige, or even a white one to match my bathroom
and was annoyed that the only ones available were various
shades of pink. Even more irritating: They cost more than men's
razors, which have more blades. It didn't make sense. So I decided to make a post on Instagram stories and tag @Target, asking them these questions directly. But instead of a reply from
the company, my followers' comments filled up my inbox: "But
more important, why are you at Target?"

A lot of my followers at that time were staunch supporters
of slow fashion. They had watched a documentary called *The
True Cost,* which exposed the realities of fast fashion in much
the same way Morgan Spurlock's *Super Size Me* revealed truths
about McDonald's. The film does a deep investigation of what
low, low prices support—like unsafe conditions, human rights
violations, child labor, and beyond. It was ugly.

Target is known for selling products at low prices, and the
way they sourced these products was not aligned with Brother
Vellies' values—so my customers were calling me out. This was
my opportunity to speak up on behalf of them, and for anyone

who does not support Target's practices. This is what you do with your seat at the table.

"Does Target have any plans to alter the business model for those people who do not feel that it is a happy place?"

Rick Gomez remained silent, which further annoyed me. He had been trying to indoctrinate us with his party line and as soon as there was pushback, he had nothing to say. I grew up in a family where debate was not seen as just healthy, but critical.

While I had stopped shopping at Target and Walmart, I was aware that both corporations were among the largest employers in the country. Yet both seemed keen on keeping wages for employees close to federally mandated minimums. I also was aware of the damage caused to mom-and-pop stores every time the big guys opened a new store in a small town and undercut pricing at local businesses. It felt like the impact on small African manufacturers when several thousand polyester T-shirts are dumped in a village. I did not voice these specific arguments that day, but they all made Rick Gomez's statement of Target being such a "great" place patently untrue in my mind.

Finally, he spoke up. "We have a lot of data," Gomez said. "People love Target."

"Okay, but what are you going to do about the fact that consumers are becoming more educated?" I asked. "They want to make sure that people aren't working in unsafe conditions. They want to shop in alignment with their values. There is a high cost associated with your low prices."

I was not mad at him as an individual. I just wanted to know what their plan was. I asked him a series of questions that boiled down to: How are you planning to grow and evolve?

If we don't ask questions, we can't expect people to develop new ways of thinking of possible answers.

I told him that I had heard that when Target did a collaboration with American designers who were manufacturing in their hometowns—say N.Y. or L.A.—it was almost always a prerequisite that the line for the big-box store was made in China or Bangladesh.

So I asked, "Does Target see the importance of buying more from American companies versus products that are made in overseas sweatshops?"

He changed the subject. It was obvious he did not want to talk about it.

It would have been easy to enjoy my seat at this table, and even agree to do a Target collab. But at that point, I had gotten into this room, so I felt I had a responsibility to shift the status quo. Rick Gomez had the power to do that, too, and I could not miss this opportunity to ask, at the very least. After my speech at the CFDA, I was focused on my own accountability, and so I asked myself: "What can I do with this access?"

Winning the Fashion Fund caused a spike in business for Brother Vellies. I now had orders for five hundred thousand dollars' worth of shoes—many from prominent retailers like Net-a-Porter, Holt Renfrew, the Webster, and Matchesfashion. We were also selling online and doing three hundred thousand dollars a year with no debt. Then we hit our first million in sales. Brother Vellies had become a real business, not just a passion project. It felt surreal.

At the Incubator, I met with several assigned mentors, including Bart Solomon, an older white man. He was the financier who reportedly helped Betsey Johnson fund her company, and his client list included Michael Kors and Marc Jacobs. So I was surprised when he showed up wearing hideous loafers and ill-fitting jeans. He reminded me of a used car salesman. I had the new collection of Brother Vellies samples lined up in my office, and the first thing he said was, "How in the world are you funding this? What do your parents do? Are they helping you?"

I cringed and explained that I sold direct-to-consumer through my website and had a special arrangement with my wholesale buyers.

"You must always be short on money," he said, intrigued. He reminded me of a creepy guy at a bar asking why you are buying your own drink.

I explained that I had close relationships with most of my retail accounts, and since Brother Vellies was a small business, they agreed to give us healthy deposits to commission the work. For example, if it was a one-hundred-thousand-dollar order, they would give me a deposit of fifty thousand dollars, which I would send to the artisans to do the job and pay for shipping. While this was not normal wholesale practice, they understood that it was the only way I could provide these particular products. I had negotiated for this on our behalf.

My new dilemma, however, was that we had just signed Net-a-Porter, who wanted to adhere to a more traditional payment schedule, where they placed the order and then paid you thirty, sixty, or ninety days after you delivered the product. In many cases, retailers will also insist that most designers take back product that does not sell, which can be devastating to a small business. While I understood how this made sense for bigger clothing corporations with large coffers and lines of credit, it made it almost impossible for a small business like mine to participate.

I was in a bind: Success can do this to a small business. I had $500,000 in orders, which meant I needed $250,000 up front, to pay the workshops to commission the work. All in all, I was $70,000 short for production. I was expecting the next $100,000 installment from the Fashion Fund on August 1. But this meant there was a six-week gap when I wasn't going to have enough money. I was starting to see that it was next to impossible to fund your way through a fashion business wholesale model without resources.

During one visit to the Incubator office, Bart said that most designers can't make it in NYC without external support.

"Come to my office," he added as he was leaving. "Maybe I can help you."

I asked my accountant if he thought it was a good idea to partner with Bart, as he had a few other clients who had worked with him. I explained my reservations.

"Well, you need to raise the money quickly," he countered. "What else are you going to do? Do you have any friends or family who can help?"

It was April and the first shipment was due to ship to retailers between August 1 and 30. I was running out of time.

So one chilly afternoon, I went to Bart's office, which was a few blocks away in the Garment District. On the elevator ride up to the twelfth floor, I was considering my options: I could simply not take the Net-a-Porter production order. That was an easy solution. But then I also thought how proud our artisans would be to have their products on that site, alongside Prada and Christian Louboutin. It would be great for Brother Vellies because more customers would discover us. And it would allow me the opportunity to work with more artisans because it was a big order of shoes. I was also thinking about my two employees, my assistant, Samantha, and Anja, who was pregnant and had left an established company to come work with me because she believed in the mission, and in me. I did not want to be in a tough financial situation where I would not be able to pay their salaries. I needed money.

When I sat down with Bart at his office that day, he explained the way he could work with me, by loaning me the money for production, and then I would reimburse him once I delivered the shoes and got paid by the retailers. He name-dropped a bunch of other designers that he had relationships with, like Cushnie et Ochs, Alexander Wang, and Jason Wu. All successful. It sounded straightforward, so I agreed to work with him and signed the contract he had drawn up on the spot.

That meeting was in May and Bart promised to advance the money in June but didn't end up wiring it to our account until early July. My delivery window to Net-a-Porter was August 1 to 30. In the fashion wholesale world, you have a delivery range, so this meant all of the items had to be delivered by the thirtieth, but not before the first because there would not be space in their warehouse. Ship windows are a critical part of fashion's ever-revolving door.

This delay caused huge issues, as I needed to first send the money to Italy, where the interior part of the heel for our fall high-heeled boots was produced, which was then sent to Ethiopia, where the rest of the boot was made. I had been working with Simone and the U.N. on skills development at a workshop in Ethiopia that was going incredibly well.

I wired the money to the workshop in Italy, and they worked around the clock but did not finish by August 1, when the country closes for the month. To make matters worse, Bart called me on August 1 asking, "When are the goods shipping?"

I was shocked and said, "We just got the money! They are still making them!"

By the time we shipped the final components needed for the shoes to the Ethiopian workshop in the beginning of September, a state of emergency had been declared in the country and everything that was in customs was either held up or looted. We were only able to ship a fraction of the half a million dollars in orders.

For a young business, it was crushing. This was supposed to be our biggest wholesale season after winning the Fashion Fund and instead we were about to be overwhelmed with canceled orders and disappointed buyers. In many ways, it seemed like people had a thin layer of doubt that I would be able to pull off working in Africa and with artisans, so it felt like a particularly brutal defeat. On top of that, I now had a loan from Bart that I was not going to be able to pay off easily. And the deposits that several stores had paid me had been sunk into making key components for those orders—including the heels, leather straps, insoles, and embellishments—that were being looted.

I was also deeply worried about the artisans in Ethiopia. While they were physically okay, I knew that they could not afford to not be working. My colleagues at the U.N. were trying to help pick up the pieces. I felt like my business was falling apart. We had fallen down, but I was determined to get back up. The only thing I could do was focus on the next scheduled collection.

It would be a resort collection, which usually delivers to stores in November in preparation for holiday vacations. That meant I needed the deposits from retailers, so I could start paying up front for those orders. When I called the retailers to let them know the plan, they told me that they had already received a call from Bart's team and had forwarded the deposits to Bart.

Confused, I called Bart: "Can you transfer those deposits? I need them so I can deliver resort on time and make up for the fall fail."

"The deposits that you received from retailers are being held in an account, in escrow," he explained in a patronizing way. "I am not going to be releasing that money until you ship fall. If you need more money for resort, we can discuss another loan."

That felt like a punch in the stomach—I literally gasped for air.

"I don't need to borrow more money," I explained. "I need my deposits."

"Well, they're in escrow, as per the contract you signed," he said. "You haven't finished delivering fall."

I hung up the phone, my shock turning to anger. He knew I couldn't deliver because of the political unrest in Ethiopia. In a flash, my mentor had turned into a piranha. I was not sure what to do. So I called my mom.

"Sounds like sharecropping," she said, and went on to explain an entire industry created in the late 1800s to keep formerly enslaved people from owning land. "Technically, they could buy land, but they would need to take out loans to help establish their crops," my mom explained. "The people who loaned them money would institute repayable terms that were next to impossible to achieve. Each time a deadline was missed, the person who issued the loan would take a little piece of land until it was all gone." I felt sick to my stomach. This seemed to be exactly what he was doing.

It was a vicious cycle, and I suddenly understood why he'd waited until July to pay me the initial deposit. He makes interest on the money held in escrow, so the longer it is there, the more money he makes. And I had signed his contract without understanding the legalese. It was the only contract I had not run by my lawyer, mostly because Bart was a mentor assigned through the CFDA. I trusted him, and I had agreed to this wildly unfair arrangement. I was so mortified and ashamed. I did not tell anyone beyond my mother and a few close friends.

Without sharing my situation, I started asking other designers what they had heard about Bart. He had a reputation for making designers sign personal guarantees. I learned that he had made a female friend of mine, Ryan Roche, take out a second mortgage on her home. She had been a runner-up in the Fashion Fund the year before me, and made beautiful classic sweaters, coats, and dresses in luxe fabrics, like silk and cashmere. I called another female designer who confided, in tears, that she was coming close to having to close her business because of a deal she had signed with Bart.

I was starting to panic: What had I gotten myself into?

Within a few months, the interest and fees on that $70,000 loan ballooned into $150,000. Around this same time, Anja became a single mom, which meant her salary, which was six figures, was a check I could not bounce. So I started paying my own rent late to make payroll. On more than one occasion, I had to make the tough choice between making payroll or paying taxes or buying my own groceries. My team won every time.

And yet Bart continued to charge me seven thousand dollars in interest and fees monthly, including a hundred dollars a month for his internet and computer paper. Within the first year of signing that contract, I fell so far behind on rent that my landlord took me to court. At least there, I was able to arrange a payment schedule without accruing interest. That felt humane compared to what Bart was doing.

Everyone in fashion talks about mentors, but no one wants to talk about the financial struggles of young designers who rack up debt with loan sharks like Bart. You cannot mentor your way out of needing capital. Once again, I saw how people like me, with no inheritance or connection to moneyed people, no family ties within the business or Harvard MBA, are vulnerable to sharks like Bart. I now know this practice is common: People like him build up huge debt with a young entrepreneur and then convert it into ultra-cheap equity, all while posing as mentors. I was embarrassed that I had been so naïve.

Financial systems are created to keep those with means with

means. It makes it very hard to participate in the American dream. The few people who came from nothing and managed to fight their way to the top are exceptional stories. Knowing all of the designers I have met over the years, there is no correlation between the ones who work the hardest, the ones who are the most talented, and the ones who are the most successful. There are no straight lines. Fashion is not the only industry set up like that.

I complained to the CFDA for being given a terrible mentor and to Lisa Smilor, the Incubator liaison. She was horrified. At one point, when I started to get evicted from the Incubator office because I had no money to pay the rent, she called Bart and he wrote a check to help cover it. And yet, when I shared the contract with my lawyer, I learned that although what Bart was doing was terrible, it was also perfectly legal—because I had signed the contract.

Meanwhile, and ironically, Brother Vellies was in the press; I had won the Fashion Fund. So everyone was so happy for me. Brother Vellies was being worn constantly by celebrities like Beyoncé, Rihanna, Zendaya, and Lady Gaga.

And I was too scared to tell anyone the truth.

Even worse, I had to see Bart every season, whenever new orders came in. That was my only chance at getting the deposits, which he was holding in escrow. This was why I found myself in a small alley on Thirty-sixth Street puking into a garbage can and trying to get control of my nerves before taking that elevator ride up to Bart's office on the twelfth floor. It reminded me of dealing with Winston: I had to maintain my composure, keep my cool, and do my best to outwit him in order to survive. It was the only way I could get money to my workshops. But his approach was to always try to get the products for cheaper. So if I had a hundred-thousand-dollar purchase order from Nordstrom, and the store would give me fifty thousand, Bart would ask, "Well, how much will it cost you to make the order?" I'd say, "Forty-seven thousand dollars." And he'd tell me, "I will give you a loan for forty thousand."

Bart's number one objective was making a profit, period. This was a third-generation business, and as long as he could continue to rationalize his situation, he would see himself as a good guy: a multi-generational garmento who was using his family's wealth to help poor talented designers like me.

"You would not be able to do this without me," he loved to say.

Had I been a person of more means, I would have been able to buy myself out of this situation and this system, which was not designed to help people without money to get ahead.

When I would visit Bart's office, he was usually flanked by his son and his nephew, who would complain about the brand and my margins, try to force me to fire Anja because she was "so expensive," and not provide or offer any meaningful advice or help.

I started looking for ways to make money that did not depend on wholesale and saw that the only way for me to fund the business and not buckle under Bart's pressure was to focus entirely on growing direct-to-consumer sales online. The timing was good because the Fashion Fund TV show had just started to air, and our web traffic and Instagram accounts were growing with each episode. I seized every opportunity to interact with my customers via Instagram, and before long, I had ten thousand followers. I also started doing monthly newsletters. That Valentine's Day, I wrote, "I am supposed to tell you what your boyfriend should buy you, but instead I am going to tell you that sometimes Valentine's Day sucks and you shouldn't spend time comparing yourself to other couples, or wishing you were in a relationship. Here are a pair of black shoes that you can buy for any occasion."

My customers appreciated my candor. They were a mix: Lots were entrepreneurial women, some who used to buy Manolo Blahniks and then decided they wanted to buy from a female designer. Some who loved the sustainable backstory, others who found me through the Fashion Fund.

My wholesale accounts were constantly fed up because we were often late in delivering orders. But what broke my heart was that they usually just assumed Africa was the problem when, in fact, it was Bart's funding delays and chokehold on the brand. I could not gather the courage to tell them the truth because I felt ashamed that I had been so badly duped—and I knew at the end of the day, they wouldn't really be able to do anything. This went on for a couple seasons: I let Bart hold all the money in escrow and worked tirelessly to fund some of the wholesale sales myself through e-commerce. But no matter what I did, I found myself in even more debt to him because I could not keep up with his interest and fees.

In the meantime, Bart was upset with me because I signed a management contract with IMG instead of his son Chase,

founder of Solomon Talent Group. I had agreed to take a meeting with him. He suggested Soho House in the Meatpacking
District and I came away positive that I was not letting another
Solomon ruin my life. Then Bart called: "I am really disappointed that you signed with IMG. Chase is the best. He bro-
kers everyone's deals. He probably could have gotten you a
collaboration with Target."

A year after I signed that contract with Bart, he announced that
he was no longer funding any manufacturing in Africa. "It is
too unstable," he said. "It's crazy over there. Look at Edun." He
was referring to the fashion brand Bono founded with his wife;
they had sold 49 percent of it to LVMH in 2009. The idea was
to make clothing in Africa, to support the economy there. But
the company wound up doing 80 percent of the manufacturing
in China because it was easier.

"If Bono and LVMH can't make it work, I don't know why
you think you are the person to do it," he said.

By that point, he had requested to pay the invoices directly—
and would charge me wire and administration fees for every
check he cut. This meant that I had to fund everything in Africa
myself.

I was able to work around this by sending money to my production manager in Italy, who would transfer it to the workshops
in Africa. Brother Vellies could have a great direct-to-consumer
season, and I could cover most of the production costs myself, but
the amount I owed Bart remained the same. It was a vicious cycle.
The one upside was that I was forced to wrap my head around all

the financials for my business. I took a crash course in different debt vehicles and investment structures.

Meanwhile, Brother Vellies shoes were in every major magazine. Many of our artisans were women who had become the breadwinners in their families. This was further proof that Brother Vellies was never about charity; it was always about meaningful employment. It was about proving that their culture was worth celebrating.

I became more and more determined to not let Bart ruin my business. This was not just about me. It was about Makeda, John, and all the artisans I was working with. I could not let Bart win.

Then Selby called me one day and said, "Did you see what Zara is doing?"

"No," I said.

She sent me an image of something they were calling the "Zara sandal," which was an exact copy of our bestselling Dhara sandal, an elegant black low-block-heeled shoe with a furry front strap. It was such a hit that we had a wait list. They were being made in our Ethiopia workshop where there was serious political unrest. I was more worried about the artisans' safety than the shoes being made on time, but grateful for the consumer interest because I knew it would have an impact on that community. I was devastated by how badly this knockoff might impact my ability to bring work to our Ethiopian artisans.

I posted an image of the Zara sandal on Instagram with the caption STOLEN FROM AFRICA and a sad emoji. A heated discussion

followed. A couple of my customers argued, "What am I supposed to do? I really love the aesthetic you created, but I can't
afford a $715 shoe. And I also want to participate in fashion."
This was a tough conversation to have. It has always bothered
me that our price points make the products inaccessible for so
many people. But it also proves all the ways in which fast fashion is unethical. It takes the nectar of a very beautiful idea and
waters it down in a way that removes the value and the purpose
from the original idea. If you replicate shoes that were created
to support artisan communities, and then flood the market with
them, you are eradicating all the goodwill that came from the
initial idea.

My response to people critical of our price points is that you
can love something but that does not give anyone the right to
steal it from you. If you buy that product, you are supporting a
system that not only copied my design work, but also had it
made in unregulated factories with cheap materials. It is unethical on many levels.

Teen Vogue and Refinery29 did stories on the Zara incident
in August 2016, but that did not stop Steve Madden from
knocking off another shoe, the Lamu sandal, that December,
when Ethiopia had just emerged from the state of emergency,
and we were working around the clock to get them to our customers.

Our Lamu sandal knockoff was the focus of Steve Madden's
new campaign. Every feather that we had meticulously dyed
using indigo, avocado skins, and local flowers had been copied
using a cheap chemical counterpart. Soon I found that posters
of my appropriated design—emblazoned with the bold, all-

caps title: WILD THINGS—were hanging in the windows of their retail stores all across the country. I felt sick.

Once again, I shared images of my original designs alongside the fakes. Refinery29 reported on it again. A few weeks later, I saw Piera Gelardi, the co-founder of that site, at the Women's March in Washington, D.C., and she told me that Steve Madden called and said if they did not take the story down, the company would pull all their advertising. I was no longer surprised by encountering bullies in the fashion industry. But I was relieved by her response: "I told him that we were not taking this story down," she said, adding, "Money silences people, but not in this case."

I couldn't walk five city blocks that summer without seeing similar rip-off styles of our shoes. But our story sparked an important conversation about the real damage of this copycat culture. It is challenging enough for artists and small businesses to get their creative work out in the world—realizing something like the Dhara or Lamu sandal in a sustainable way is a true labor of love. It takes time, imagination, and hard work to use elements—whether fur or feathers—that are revered parts of the communities in which these shoes are created. Each piece is made with care and attention, which takes time.

So when H&M and Zara and Shein appropriate the designs and creativity from other brands and produce them for significantly less, and often in sweatshops, it is incredibly detrimental to those original creatives. To exploit the fact that my lead times are longer because we're training people to make things, often in impoverished communities, is unethical. Even more perverse is the fact that major corporations can do this because they have the money to do so quickly and cheaply, with no repercussions.

Having cheap knockoffs ready faster than we could get our own sandals made did not just steal our design but robbed us of the full potential of what that design could have achieved by flooding the market with much-lower-priced, cheaply made versions. It is such a terrible catch-22: They reduced the value of and demand for what we were making, which in turn caused people to question our price point, which had been developed in order to pay artisans fairly, and took job opportunities from our artisans by flooding the market with the sweatshop versions. Steve Madden sold thousands of pairs of shoes that were initially designed by me; had those shoes been created by women in Ethiopia, it would have contributed thousands if not millions of dollars to their local economy.

Obviously, this is one tiny example of a David versus Goliath system, and one that devours companies like Brother Vellies often. What consumers must understand is that this is so much more than the "how to dress for less" stories we are inundated with on fashion sites. The media companies that run those stories perpetuate this system too. That narrative feeds the notion that a lower price is the goal, versus promoting a conversation about who made the product and how is it relevant to the way you live your life. The media has trained customers to expect sales and demand discounts. I am more interested in getting people to ask, "What is the intrinsic value of this object? What and who am I supporting when I pay this much money for a thing?"

· · ·

In between the Zara and Steve Madden issues, Selby called me to say that she had just seen Prada's latest collection and there were "tributes" to Brother Vellies.

"You should be flattered!" she said. "Prada is chic."

"I don't think it's chic," I countered. "I think it sucks any way you slice it."

She was quiet for a moment and then agreed. "Yeah, you are right."

Rather than fight the impossible—if not Prada, then Gucci, if not Steve Madden, then Zara—I focused on designing shoes. I've always given myself the title of creative director rather than designer because it allows space for other people to be involved in the design. I've also had to design within the confines of what was possible for our artisan communities and what was affordable given our budget. The goal for me has always been to make items that would be passed down, a woman's first splurge when she finally lands her dream job, shoes that her daughter might gleefully uncover in her closet a decade later and wear to her prom.

So when a journalist from *Condé Nast Traveler* asked me what I thought my customers liked the most about Brother Vellies, I thought about all the ways in which my brand was so different from others. For example, we work with people in actual tribes, instead of referring to our customers as our "tribe"; we weave patterns on kilns, instead of printing them on pesticide-laden cotton. But instead of getting too specific, I said: "People are looking for transparency. They want corporations to take some responsibility and accountability for their actions. When you purchase something from someone, that money changing hands is also an exchange of power. We need to make sure we empower the right people and right projects. Africa is a beautiful continent with a million stories to tell. I'm proud to have a brand that empowers artisans across Africa as opposed to just taking inspiration from them."

I wanted to grow the business so we could hire and support more artisans. It made me sick that every single dollar coming in from all of our retailers was still going to Bart. My only way out was to slowly withdraw from wholesale and figure out a way to pay him off. That meant keeping just a handful of smaller retailers that I would provide with shoes every season. They would then send the payment directly to Bart, slowly chipping away at an extraordinarily large and growing boulder. If I could not grow our sales the way I wanted to, I was determined to grow our influence for the better. I was playing the long game, which meant trying to stay true to myself and my mission. Knowing that Brother Vellies might never make it out of his grasp financially, I needed to recalibrate what kind of growth I wanted the brand to have. I wanted our brand to make sure we left our mark, in some way.

Another decision I made was to not chase celebrities for the sole purpose of getting them to wear Brother Vellies. This approach is the oldest trick in the book and a surefire one that has helped many brands. But those alignments are often inauthentic and transactional. That said, Beyoncé is Beyoncé and I was elated the day she stepped out wearing a Brother Vellies handbag.

I still received a push notification every time anyone bought anything from our online store. I was fanatically interested in speaking to my customers and learning what they wanted, liked, or disliked. That connection and sense of community is the heartbeat that keeps Brother Vellies going. That ability to connect inspired our move from the tiny South Street Seaport store to a large, airy corner store in Greenpoint, Brooklyn, with two walls of glass.

Despite all this, there were days when our debts to Bart would weigh more heavily. Would I ever be able to climb my way out? Was it worth it? And then I would see a pair of Vellies on a musician in *Vogue* and remember first meeting John in South Africa, where he had been making these shoes for generations. For him, and the artisans, to see these shoes make their way onto the pages of major magazines and be lauded and worn by celebrities was huge. I also noticed the impact on the communities every time I visited the workshops: Where there once stood an empty parking lot, there was now a pile of bicycles parked outside, and some days even a car. These jobs meant steady incomes and basic life improvements. Occasionally, I'd hear that someone was leaving the workshop to start their own business and my heart would burst: It was working.

John let me know that locally Vellies were considered fashionable again. That had always been a goal, ever since the very early days of Brother Vellies. On one trip to South Africa, back in 2012, I was wearing Vellies. A man stopped me at the airport and said, "You are such a pretty girl. You obviously have money. Why are you wearing these poor people shoes?" Meanwhile, he was wearing Nike sneakers, an Aeropostale T-shirt, and tight-fitting knockoff True Religion jeans. I thought that if we could introduce and elevate the status of Vellies in the Western world, maybe we could redefine what they meant here, in their place of origin. The West has done so much to tell the whole world what they need to wear, who they need to be idolizing, what movies they need to be watching. So much so that this man was proudly wearing an Aeropostale T-shirt—while looking down on a luxury product that was created by his own people.

Finally, six years later, I saw signs my hypothesis was being proven. Some of the older workshops that had been closed were reopening their doors. The editor in chief of *Elle South Africa* reached out and flew to Brooklyn to have a meeting with me. We became fast friends. This was about communities being supported, and their indigenous shoe shapes being appreciated in new ways. Whatever strife I was having with Bart paled in comparison.

Brother Vellies was leaving a mark.

I was so thrilled when Stella, an intern turned full-time employee, asked for the opportunity to usher in a new category of shoes: huaraches. This was a shoe that I grew up with and loved. Stella was born and raised in Mexico and knew of a multi-generational workshop in Chiapas that had been making that shoe for decades. So when she asked if she could spearhead the project, I was entirely on board.

I share a lot of my thinking behind the design process on my personal Instagram account to show customers how things are made. Our average price point is high, so it is helpful to show the production process to our community: how it takes hours to carve the wood handles on our Nile bags, or intricately dye and stitch feathers, one by one, on a handcrafted bridal shoe.

Fast fashion survives by dehumanizing the process. If we as-

sume that a machine is able to create a Steve Madden shoe for
$19.99, then we don't have to ask questions about any of the
people and the wages that were involved in sourcing the leather,
making the rubber sole, stitching the seams, and assembling the
final shoe, when the laces are threaded eyelet by eyelet and tied
into a perfect bow. If we assume that a living wage is even just
$10 an hour, then what must all these people be getting paid in
order for Steve Madden to sell a shoe for just $19.99 and still be
making over $100 million in profit every year?

Meanwhile, Bart kept pressuring me to sell at Urban Outfit-
ters or Anthropologie to help service my mounting debt—to
him. He even suggested that I move my production to China.
And despite my determination, by the end of 2017, I remained
in so much debt my accountant suggested closing the brand.

"You won the Fashion Fund," he said. "You can go get a six-
figure salary working for Tory Burch." But this was not just
about me. And it was not just about selling shoes. There was a
bigger purpose behind the things I was making, and I refused to
stop.

16

Close to the Sun

Then, in January 2018, Donald Trump called Haiti a shit-
hole country. I was so upset the day Hillary Clinton lost
that I marched to Trump Tower in the rain, destroying my hand-
carved high-heeled Moroccan clogs along the way, screaming
my head off. I had campaigned for Hillary. I liked Bernie Sand-
ers, too—his policies reminded me of growing up in Canada—
but in the end, I decided to put my energy and voice behind
Hillary because I wholeheartedly believed that she was the most
qualified person to ever run for president, and I believed in her
ability to get great work done.

Our newsletters were growing more political, as we were
now working in Africa, Haiti, Italy, and Mexico, and I responded to Trump's racism with a piece that was in direct op-
position to his quote. But I also knew there are many ways to

protest and sometimes just existing in your joy is the strongest form of that. So, I continued to make beautiful shoes and share beautiful stories about our artisans and these countries that have endured so much.

My customers cared deeply about these stories, so much so that I have never had to spend money on advertising campaigns. Our direct-to-consumer sales just kept growing via social media. We had a loyal following, including Meghan Markle, who spent the summer of 2018 wearing our huaraches. We quickly sold out of the hundred pairs we had in stock and grew a wait list of several thousand people. There were many occasions over the years where we could have sold exponentially more product, but because of my own lack of capital, even when we had a style that truly took off, we usually only had twenty to thirty pairs on hand to sell.

It was around this time that more people started talking about diversity on the runway, and asking, "Is that brand diverse? How many Black models walked in that show?" Meanwhile, some of the brands that would use the most Black models on their runways were putting Black women in grave jeopardy in their factories—creating a cognitive dissonance and dangerous optical allyship. Your choice to give one woman five hundred dollars to walk in your fashion show has nothing to do with your company culture and business practices as a whole.

It was becoming abundantly clear to me that companies that don't grow with the times will eventually age themselves out of relevancy. It can't just be about hiring Black models. Fashion brands also need to be actively recruiting from HBCUs, taking on interns from diverse backgrounds, and creating retail-to-

corporate pipeline programs to create upward mobility for retail staff who may not be in a position to go to a fancy fashion
school or do a summer internship for free in NYC. In my own
experience, some of the coolest people who work for a brand
are in their retail stores and not on their corporate staff. It made
me wonder how much companies miss out on by not creating
more internal opportunities. I was excited to grow Brother Vellies so I could test out some of my own theories on inclusivity.

Managing a small but growing business on a shoestring budget was challenging to say the least. And there were days where
I couldn't help but dream about what it would be like to have all
of the resources a brand like Edun had with backing from
LVMH, or a team of thirty-five people. And anyone coming up
in fashion in New York has heard the fairy-tale story of how
Barneys bought Proenza Schouler's entire first collection, right
after they had graduated from Parsons. But what if you couldn't
afford to go to Parsons? Or what if Barneys knocked off your
design in their private line because you were not as marketable
as the Proenza duo? Or what if you were not being seen by retail buyers who understood what your products actually stood
for? I often got feedback from department stores that the brand
was too "raw and complicated." And I cannot tell you how
often Brother Vellies was described as urban.

And yet, Brother Vellies was gaining more attention and
customers and acclaim. I had already been named Footwear
News Emerging Talent of the year in 2015. And then in 2018,
I was nominated for the CFDA Swarovski Award for Emerging
Talent. So it was understandable why Bart kept asking me why
the orders from major retailers weren't increasing. But by 2019,

I had stopped selling to large retailers almost entirely. We simply couldn't afford to do it. Often their teams wouldn't take the time to understand the price points and materials and would place us in the cheaper shoe section, instead of the space I felt made sense. Bart was keeping the deposits, so we had to fund orders by ourselves, or with more loans from him—and he would keep 100 percent of the resulting sales too.

And yet, that same year, *Time* included me among thirty-four optimists "changing how we see our world," and the Canada Arts and Fashion Awards gave me the International Canadian Designer Award. I spoke in my acceptance speech of how heavily I relied on my Canadian upbringing to make choices that took everyone's well-being into consideration.

In some ways, it was hard to receive accolades when the business was in such a tough financial position. But it has also always given me hope for the future. People were acknowledging the value of the work. I remember thinking, even if Brother Vellies did not work out, at least I had changed people's minds about what it meant to be made in Africa and that sustainability did not have to be relegated to the crunchy corners of the earth and can really be a luxury proposition.

Receiving those recognitions fueled my resolve, and despite all the challenges, the brand was growing stronger. Our direct-to-consumer sales were taking off, and we had strong margins and a diverse supply chain spanning from New York to Nairobi. If I closed my eyes and pretended my financial issues did not exist, we were winning. So, I decided to stay my course.

. . .

In mid-April 2018, I got a phone call from Solange's publicist, Janna.

"Solange wants to go to the Met Gala with you," she explained. It had never occurred to me, until that very moment, that I would ever even attend the Met Gala.

The gala is a fundraiser for the Metropolitan Museum of Art in New York City and kicks off an exhibit each year that focuses on a specific theme or designer. I remember going to see the Costume Institute exhibit on a school field trip when I was fifteen and falling in love with Alexander McQueen and Vivienne Westwood. The theme that year was "Heavenly Bodies: Fashion and the Catholic Imagination." As someone who grew up going to museums and church, it felt full circle.

I had become friends with Solange through the Okpo sisters and she was a huge supporter of the brand. I love that she is unapologetically Black, and her songs highlight her unique point of view as a Black woman. She had recently released one of my favorite albums, *A Seat at the Table*.

It seemed far-fetched that I could get tickets to the most coveted event of the year. But I told her I would try.

Anna Wintour is responsible for the invite list every year. But what most people don't realize is that the Met Gala is the sole source of funding for the Metropolitan Museum's Costume Institute. The museum is free and open to the public 362 days per year. So there is a large price tag attached to every seat at the gala.

I decided to write to Anna. I told her that seeing Solange and me there would mean so much to other young women who look like us. I had nothing to lose and hit send on the email.

Anna and I had stayed in touch after the Fashion Fund. She checked in on me regularly, featured the brand more than anyone else, and frequently invited me to a myriad of different events, from political fundraisers to dinners supporting the Youth Anxiety Center. She had even pushed for me to assume a creative director role for LVMH designing the brand Edun, a job I *did* want. I had proven that luxury made in Africa was possible and imagined all the amazing things I could do with LVMH's resources behind me. I threw my heart into that application, creating beautiful mood boards, sending in portfolios and sketches as well as sourcing and production plans. Anna told me that she was personally rooting for me. After six months of determined work, in the end, they never hired anyone. The company never took off, and to this day, Rihanna is the only Black female creative director at LVMH.

Invites for the Met Gala go out in December. This was late April, and the event happens the first Monday in May. I knew it was a long shot, but I also knew it could be another milestone moment for Brother Vellies if we attended. Anna responded immediately and supportively. Once someone from her team wrote back to say tickets were secured, I was both thrilled and nervous. What was I signing up for?

I immediately started making accessories for Solange, who was, at the time, interested in Florida Water, said to be blessed by shamans. So I also designed and wove a hand-beaded Swarovski crystal bag, made of two thousand crystals, to carry her Florida Water.

Solange settled on a black latex dress by Iris van Herpen, which she wore with a Black du-rag and a headpiece created by the hairstylist Jawara that looked like a halo of braided hair. To complement that look, I made custom latex thigh-high Brother Vellies heels. I wanted to make my own dress but ran out of time.

Solange's stylist had long acrylic nails that click-clacked as we tried on shoe after shoe all week during fittings. And then the afternoon of the Met Gala, as we were putting the final touches on a fully perfected look, one of those long red nails sliced through the entire front of the smooth black latex of the sandal sock. We all stood in shock, jaws on the floor, looking at the shoe massacre in front of us. In a panic, I sent my assistant to scour every aisle of every kink store in Chelsea to find another latex sock to replace it.

When we finally made it to the red carpet, with ten minutes to spare, my adrenaline was still coursing. But I looked around and saw many familiar faces. All the designers looked a little bit nervous too. The Met is a big stage. They are artists after all, and this was the night where there are a lot of questions asked, like: What do you have to say about the world at that moment? About religion? About Catholicism? And symbolism? This night was about fashion as expression, as conversation, as art: the way my mother had taught me to respect and revere it.

Solange was making a bold statement: Her God was most definitely Black. I'm sure that made people uncomfortable. But she was going to be her beautiful, brilliant, creative self, which is what has always made her so great.

The headlines from the night were amusing: SOLANGE BRINGS UNKNOWN BLACK DESIGNER TO MET GALA. But they eventually brought great recognition for the brand and helped us reach

new audiences. I understood how crucial it was for a Black female designer to attend an event like that. Those Brother Vellies
shoes were the only items made by a Black woman who walked
the red carpet that night.

When I learned that the theme for the Met Gala in 2019 was
"Camp," inspired by an essay penned by Susan Sontag in 1964
called "Notes on 'Camp,'" I wrote Anna again to say that I
wanted to come, but I disagreed with Sontag, who claimed that
camp was man-made, not natural. She was speaking about people who had access to man-made synthetic materials—sequins,
Swarovski crystals, and tulle. Meanwhile, throughout my travels in Africa, I was constantly struck by how the most outra-
geous and campiest things *are* natural. Leopard and zebra prints
are obvious examples, but also, isn't an orchid the campiest
beauty of all?

I had been using a lot of raffia for Brother Vellies and studying ritualistic costumes from Benin, made of the straw-like material in elaborately braided huts, that priests wear for specific
ceremonies. I wanted to riff on that idea for my dress and started
making a corset top woven out of the material. In my research,
I came across the artist Simone Yvette Leigh, whose work is a
profound meditation on Black women and our bodies. She
made one sculpture of a woman wearing a tiered skirt made of
straw, like the costumes I had seen in Benin, which inspired me
to reach out to her for advice. She was so generous and kind,
responding enthusiastically with suggestions and notes on how
to make such a garment.

I also started working on the chain for the bag I would carry
that was hand-carved on the coast of Kenya from a single piece

of wood. All the links were solid and maintained their structural integrity. I wore my hair in box braids, with beads sourced from throughout Africa—hand-batiked wood, pieces of sea amber from Guinea-Bissau, pearl agate beads, beads formed from natural tree sap in a deep amber, and light sandalwood beads. The goal was to represent African craftsmanship and illustrate how natural materials play a vital role in fashion as the inspiration for so many synthetic versions we would also be seeing on the carpet.

That year, my dress got a lot of attention. It was different, it was loud, it was camp. It was also fun—albeit incredibly uncomfortable as the corset was also made of rigid straw pieces that javelined my stomach every time I tried to sit down.

I was about to turn thirty-five and had done quite well achieving the goals I had in terms of business and fashion. Following my breakup with Jason, I dated a stylist for years, and that relationship had also come to an end. But I was starting to question what else I wanted in my life. Did I want to be a mother? Could I do both? I would have these long conversations with my dear friend Mia Moretti, who suggested I go to the Hoffman Institute. She had gone the year before at the suggestion of her best friend, Katy Perry, and described it as a grounding experience that gave her clarity about where to focus her energy. Shortly thereafter, I was having dinner with my friend Sade Lythcott, whose mother started the National Black Theater. Sade had gone, as well. "It is a must," she said.

The Hoffman Institute offers a seven-day retreat, no TV, no

newspapers, no working out. You meet in big and small groups, sometimes there is conversation, sometimes there is not. The whole idea is to re-center yourself. Considering you are only allowed to go once in your life, this felt like the time I needed to go. That was where I learned about geese.

17

Homesick for another World

I arrived in White Sulphur Springs in Northern California on
January 3, 2020, to do a weeklong intensive of small group
circles and one-on-one discussions with everyone from a psy-
chologist to various artists to a rabbi from Israel. It was a time to
meditate and interrogate who I was and why I did what I did,
for better or for worse.

During the week, I had an epiphany: It is hard to hold people responsible for your disappointment if you never make a
clear ask for what you need. I promised myself that I would be
more articulate about what I needed moving forward, especially if I planned on blaming anyone else for my feelings. At
the end of the week, I learned about geese.

Geese fly in a V formation to make it easier for the flock to
move forward. The birds in the back use the momentum gener-

ated by the wings of those flying in front of them. Each bird cycles through the pattern: The one in the front eventually winds up in the back, floating on the currents created by the work being done by others. It's an instinctual mechanism that helps geese lighten the load for one another.

The constant quacking you hear when geese are flying is the back of the flock cheering on the ones in the front, who are working the hardest. And if, at any point, a goose has an issue and starts to drop out of the V, two others will drop with the tired or distressed bird so they're always able to carry that V. They will stay together in a mini V of three until that goose recovers or dies. If it passes away, the other two will wait for another formation of geese and join their V.

This practice made so much sense to me: We're meant to be in community and sometimes it's critical for us to carry the load for one another. It is also impossible to go very far alone. We travel best with the momentum of others and our voices are best heard in a chorus. I did not realize then how the flight patterns of geese would guide the biggest choices of my life.

Following a week of deep reflection, I came back home to Brooklyn with the resolve to make clear asks—for myself and for Brother Vellies. I was determined to grow the business, and maybe even find my dream investor.

I went to Milan in early February for its fashion week and everyone was talking about this mysterious virus. I was already paranoid about the spread of infectious disease. Ebola reached its peak just as I was starting Brother Vellies, back in 2015.

While that was contained to West Africa, the one everyone was talking about in Milan sounded so eerily familiar that Mia and I decided to leave early.

At the airport, there were men in hazmat suits taking our temperatures before we boarded our plane.

I sat stoic in Paris at the Dior show as models in elaborate gowns marched down the runways wearing slogans like WE SHOULD ALL BE FEMINISTS in big bold writing as though they were going to war in what we hoped would be the final year of the Trump presidency. Cameras flashed; people cheered. I was in a sea of familiar faces, packed in like sardines. The designer Sami Miro was seated next to me. We smiled at each other after the finale.

"It's good to see you!" she said, above the din of applause and chatter.

"Likewise," I responded. "Hope to see you soon!"

Little did we know that we would not be together again in a room like this for years.

When I left, street-style photographers were running around frantically, capturing the dazzle of women flocking out of the space. The dissonance was heavy: Word of the coronavirus was spreading, but fashion week continued to press on. People were already dying from Covid, in not-so-faraway places, and yet it seemed as if no one here cared.

Once back in Brooklyn, I learned that two of my shop employees had fallen sick—neither of whom had traveled to Europe with me. I closed the Brother Vellies office immediately, worried first and foremost about my team, which by then had grown to five people. No one else seemed too concerned in

New York, where the streets were bustling, neighbors chatting on stoops and in expensive cafés, glasses clinking, living life as usual. But I couldn't ignore the foreboding I felt, fueled by the news coming from the workshops in Italy of rising cases there and in other parts of Europe. It all made me uneasy.

And then, on March 20, Governor Cuomo issued the shelter-in-place mandate. But before I shut myself into a small apartment like the rest of New York City, I left the house one final time with my friend Kerby. We needed to stock up on essentials for ourselves, and his aunt. She was older and he wanted to ensure that she did not have any reason to go out. Kerby and I had met at the Incubator, and he is now one of my very best friends. He takes incredible care of the people he loves. His aunt was not home when we arrived but pulled up a few minutes later. She explained that she had gone to a Verizon store to get her phone fixed. Kerby was distraught, with good reason. She got sick shortly thereafter.

Ambulance sirens filled the otherwise silent streets, a shrieking backdrop to the anxiety we were all feeling. For that reason, it did not even occur to me to check on my own company's sales. But roughly ten days into that citywide stay-at-home order, I saw they had dropped by 90 percent. My heart dropped too. I was torn, because the last thing I wanted to do was tell my customers to buy shoes, but I was also afraid that everything I had worked so incredibly hard for was going to disappear. I was also worried about my assistants who were ill, and all the artisans that Brother Vellies worked with as it was already clear that this virus was going to have a global impact.

Meanwhile, I was getting bombarded in my inbox by sales

and promotional newsletters from so many other fashion brands—their panicky reaction to the industry's plummet in revenue. I was also seeing swaths of people in fashion get laid off. I knew I needed to be reacting to the humanity of this moment. As a luxury brand, I wanted to give my customers the luxury of not putting capitalism first. From the very beginning, Brother Vellies' mission had been to support people. That was being tested like never before. Plus, we were still not receiving any of our wholesale payments, as they were still going to Bart. The business was surviving on its direct-to-consumer sales. I wanted to take my time to consider what I could offer my customers at this moment.

Thankfully, the two women who worked at the Greenpoint store, Grace and Stella, recovered from Covid, but so many people in New York City and beyond did not. That spring was nightmarish. We lost Kerby's aunt, and I am still grappling with the enormity of that. People were glued to their devices, looking for any glimmer of hope, finding none, panicking.

I promised myself that I wouldn't lay anyone off or cut their pay. The CFDA worked quickly to distribute a pattern to make masks, which I sent over to the workshops along with several thousand dollars. My grandmother always told me that the most important time to give was when it felt the hardest. Now was one of those hardest moments. On April 18, I posted a shot of a woman in our Kenyan workshop making masks using whatever material we could get access to.

I was also, like many, trapped at home. My daily meditation became making my coffee. Right before the pandemic, I had visited Oaxaca with one of my best friends, the artist Hugo

McCloud, to research a potential project for the Whitney Museum of American Art. I was excited. There I met several ceramic artisans, one of whom was a woman named Macrena. She made beautiful items out of gorgeous dark red-brown Oaxacan clay, including the mug that now held the swirl of my fresh brewed coffee. I loved to watch as the almond milk I splashed in it every morning created a kaleidoscope of earth-toned hues, from walnut to oak to sand, until they all mixed together to create the perfect caramel. It was so beautiful that I made a small video to share with my followers. That same day, several DMed me: "Where did you get that gorgeous mug?"

That gave me an idea: I reached out to Macrena to see what her production capacity was, and she said she could make five a day safely at home. That inspired me to start a "Bodega" section on the Brother Vellies website where I could sell one-off items, like coffee mugs or placemats. Items that artisans could make in addition to shoes. I also thought I could use that space to start to sell some of my own belongings if things got really tough. I was willing to do anything to keep the company afloat. I began a mental inventory of things I could part with in order to make payroll.

Before the pandemic, I had been working on developing socks at a factory in Georgia. I have always been a sock fanatic and believe they can serve as the perfect punctuation point to the right shoe moment. I also knew people would take more comfort in cozy, cotton slouchy socks than knee-high boots at that moment. I designed what became our "cloud" socks, an instant hit. For the launch, we gave all of our proceeds to our African artisans to help them make and distribute masks.

I had also kept in touch with a brilliant Tamil man named Dileepan, whom I met at Hoffman and who worked in tech and had an MBA from Harvard. He had a lot of insight into how to run a business. One night, while talking with him on the phone, I asked how his clients were faring.

"Some are crushing it," he said.

"What's the common denominator?" I asked.

"Subscriptions," he said. "Any of the wellness brands running a subscription model are printing money right now."

A lightbulb went on: I had artisans who could not work because the global supply chain had shut down. I also had these incredible women who followed me on social media trapped at home, dying to connect with the outside world. And I needed to make sure Brother Vellies had recurring revenue so I could keep paying my staff. How could I take these three unique issues and create one beautiful solution? That was how "Something Special" was born.

I started with the Oaxacan mug, which led me to think: "What if I ask all of the artisans I already work with to make items for the home?" Mugs, wooden utensils, woven baskets, braided sweetgrass: The possibilities were endless. And on April 21, 2020, I launched Something Special, a monthly subscription of handmade home items for thirty-five dollars, with this post: "I created @BrotherVellies with the intention of bringing more beauty into the world by supporting artisan Communities of Color across the globe. To navigate this difficult time in our world, I've leaned on the mission that's guided me all along. What's brought me the most joy despite the uncertainty has been making special things for you. New things. In

little batches. Each made with love by our Artisan community
for you to enjoy at home."

As I was developing the idea, I was growing more and more
excited at what this could mean for Brother Vellies' entire
community—from the artisans to the customers. Commission-
ing artisans to create products for the home with love and care;
utilizing local, slow, sustainable sourcing; and offer these things
on a monthly basis meant a steady income for the artisans and a
reliable source of revenue for the company. It was a win-win,
and the first time we had ever been able to offer artisan-made
items at this price point on our site. I wanted to help create and
share items that were made thoughtfully, with love, that would
bring joy to everyone involved. That was my definition of luxury, an idea that is not represented solely by a price point, but
by a process. I knew my community would understand—and
they did.

Within a month, one thousand people signed up. That led us
to commission artisans in Kenya to carve fifteen hundred
wooden key chains for another offering, and several indigenous
women's groups to handpick and braid sweetgrass with an intoxicating aroma for another. Within two months, the program
grew to twenty-five hundred subscribers. Meanwhile, headlines
were reporting how the fashion industry was flailing due to the
pandemic and factories were going out of business because retailers were canceling orders. That meant people were out of
work at a time when steady income was vital. I understood then
that having a direct and transparent relationship with my customers gave me autonomy. And this gave me hope: It was possible to rework old systems and build new norms.

The subscriptions quickly surpassed the need for the Bodega, which meant I never had to sell any of my personal belongings. Plus, most subscribers were first-time customers who liked the brand but found the higher price points hard to access, which was exciting.

I knew if we started ingraining these everyday objects into people's spaces—sweetgrass, coffee mugs, coconut fiber doormats, shea butters—it might help them start thinking differently about all of the objects that they potentially want to bring into their space, and how those can be sourced in a way that supports collectives and craftspeople who uplift their own communities. It must never be forgotten that as consumers with very real spending power, our actions hold great weight.

That May, *Harper's Bazaar* asked me to write about Something Special, which I was happy to do as I saw how it was a metaphor for what so many of us needed at that moment. I felt that people could and should use their money wisely, to support companies that were actively doing good in the world. Fast fashion is made generally by the hands of women, usually of color. "When you force women to work for you for free that is slavery," I wrote. I was not pulling any punches. "And for what? A blouse from a fast-fashion brand we saw an influencer post? I am not saying all of this to be negative. I am sharing it because it is a reality and since we are at this crucial fork in the road we deserve to know the true nature of the climate we are living in. Fight hard for the things you believe in."

Then, on May 25, 2020, George Floyd was murdered.

18

My ask

Suddenly, the quiet streets of Brooklyn were filled with protestors, placards, drumbeats, and megaphones. I understood the impulse. I had been doing so much marching during the Trump years. But I was also exhausted, tired of shouting, pleading for justice, making posters, and signing petitions. I could not put my body in the street this time. I wanted to do something different. I just was not sure what that was exactly.

On May 28, I was in my apartment, arranging white lilies, the most elegant flowers sold at my bodega on the corner of Bedford Avenue and Monroe. Once again, I found myself seeking solace in plants. I always come back to what they teach us. You need healthy soil, exposure to sunlight, the right amount of water—not too much or too little—and opportunity. With the correct ratios, you get to witness the most magnificent

transformation, from seed to sprout to bud to bloom. I was reminded of this possibility with every lily stem I placed in my
Oaxacan earth-brown vase, breathing in its sweet scent as Nina
Simone's voice echoed through a small speaker in my living
room: "When you feel really low, there's a great truth that you
should know."

Many people had reached out to me since the protests began,
wondering what they could do. White people, in particular,
were feeling a sense of urgency. They wanted to do something
to help, in many ways, to stop themselves from feeling like they
were part of the problem. But their Malcolm X quotes and
Black square Instagram posts felt hollow. I could not help but
think all these good intentions did not save George Floyd, or
the countless Black people murdered before him. So I just stayed
quiet. I stayed indoors. And I arranged beautiful bodega flowers
into sweet-smelling bouquets.

As I snipped and placed another stem, I heard a low rumble
outside. It sounded like thunder in the distance. Then, I heard
voices: a murmur layered on top of a pounding. Soon, I could
decipher the chant, "No justice, no peace," above a rhythmic
drumbeat. The sounds poured through my open windows,
quickly drowning out Nina's voice. I looked outside to see my
street packed with people and posters. The crowd was both
angry and vibrant. Their movement felt as if it had a magnetic
current coursing through it. I understood why they were there
and was incredibly grateful. But I did not want to join them. I
needed to do it differently this time.

I finished an arrangement, placed it on my dining room
table, and poured myself a glass of orange wine. As I sat in my

living room, listening to the cacophony outside, I thought about what it meant to be in community at this moment. I was also trying to understand what action would feel intuitive versus reactionary. Too often, there is pressure to do what everyone else is doing. I wanted to pause and really consider: How do I feel? What do I want to do? How can I harness this energy? Not just for me, but for Black people?

These thoughts were tumbling through my head as I went to bed that evening, windows open, letting the sound of other people demanding justice lull me to sleep.

The next morning, my phone jolted me awake. It was my friend calling. She had a partnership with Target. The company's use of diversity in marketing still felt like a ploy, like optical allyship, to me.

I loved and admired my friend, but I was disappointed in her for partnering with them. And yet I knew that it was not her fault. I wrestled with this internally: She is a Black woman who has worked incredibly hard to navigate a tricky media landscape to get where she is. Is it fair or right to suggest that a Black woman not take a big check after we have been historically excluded from creating generational wealth? But then again, as Black women, do we go against our better judgment and just take the check because we know if we don't, someone else will? At what point do we exercise our own privilege, which we have worked so hard to achieve, to draw a line in the sand and stop advocating for institutions that may not deserve our favor?

She knew how I felt about Target, so I was surprised that she wanted to talk to me about what the company could do in response to George Floyd's murder.

"They are based in Minneapolis," she said.

I did not want to problem-solve for Target, and the fact that my friend, who always fights the good fight, was helping this particular company at this particular moment, upset me.

"Aurora, they want to help," she insisted.

I stayed silent, but my head was beginning to spin with all the ways I potentially disagreed with that statement.

"They want to respond to this moment," she said. "The company is run by great people!"

I took a breath before I said, "Of course, the employees can be wonderful people and still work at a corporation that is inherently racist."

"What! They do a lot for the community!" she said. "They are about to make a two-million-dollar donation to the NAACP!"

"Two million does not come close to how much money Black people spend in *any* given morning at their stores," I replied. "They're not doing enough."

"But they have all these Black beauty brands," she countered.

This further enraged me. "Why wouldn't they? That just sounds like good business. Am I supposed to be grateful? That they want to sell to us? Being open to taking our money does not make them anti-racist!"

Silence fell over our call.

"Besides, how many of the brands they are marketing to us are actually Black owned?"

"I don't know," she said. "Maybe four?"

"Four . . . out of thousands!" I retorted.

She, understandably, was beginning to get frustrated with me and we both hung up agitated. My issues with Target might seem petty compared to the gross injustice of police brutality. But I was starting to sense it was connected. I just was not sure how, yet. I thought back to meeting Rick Gomez, Target's chief marketing officer, who spoke to me and the other fellows at the CFDA Incubator. He kept insisting, "Everyone loves Target!"

The pink-razor moment—and the critique from my followers, who believe so deeply in sustainability and community, who are macro thinkers—helped me understand, at the time, the guilty feeling I got every time I shopped there. I knew that I was participating in the universally accepted American obsession with cheaper, faster, happier. I also knew that Target had the power to change the narrative at this moment.

Then, it dawned on me: These retailers cannot exist without the support of Black spending dollars. They were all making million-dollar donations to Black Lives Matter causes—but this was not the most effective way they could be supporting Black people. Every stat I read about Covid's impact on Black-owned businesses was another example of systemic racism, whether it was that over 40 percent were closing due to the pandemic— compared to 17 percent of white-owned businesses—or that 70 percent of us (including me) were left behind in the first round of PPP. It started to feel personal and avoidable.

I thought back to all the challenges I had experienced with my company. I'd believed that they were simply because I was not a good businessperson. I'd convinced myself that I was not as smart as Sophia Amoruso. Or as well connected as Audrey

Gelman, who co-founded the Wing. Or I did not have a résumé like Emily Weiss, who interned at Ralph Lauren and *Teen Vogue* before launching Glossier; or business acumen like Sara Blakely, who founded Spanx. These are all incredibly complicated female entrepreneurs—and yet, pre-pandemic, they graced the covers of dozens of business magazines.

I launched my business with thirty-five hundred dollars of my own savings at the flea market on the Lower East Side of Manhattan. My story may have looked like theirs in that I won awards and received a lot of press, but every single step of growing my business had been a struggle—to the point that I had contemplated closing Brother Vellies on several occasions. I also knew that I had to fight infinitely harder than my white male peers: I did not have "friends and family" investors, or a Harvard MBA. When I started Brother Vellies, I didn't even have a credit history. And to this day, Brother Vellies still does not have its own dedicated line of credit. It took me years to get a Capital One card with a five-hundred-dollar limit.

I did a quick search online and learned that white people make up 61 percent of the U.S. population, but their businesses yield 82 percent of all the revenue earned across the entire country. They hold 81 percent of all board and 92.6 percent of all CEO positions at Fortune 500 companies. The BIPOC comparisons for heads of company are 1 percent Black, 2.6 percent Indian or East Asian, and 3.4 percent Latinx.

To have all these big companies scrambling to connect with any Black person they knew for ideas on how to support the Black community disheartened me. All they had done to date was place more Black and brown people in ad campaigns and

Instagram posts. It was not enough. Now, in May 2020, due to yet another horrific loss within the Black community, companies were finally being pressured to say "Black lives matter" out loud. They were giving large donations to Black activist groups. But they had not yet looked at supporting Black people via Black-owned businesses or changing any of their own structures or processes.

#DefundthePolice was the main conversation during those days, but I was beginning to see how it was all connected. We were talking about racial justice, but not how it applied to economic justice. Meanwhile, companies had long been clamoring to participate in "social entrepreneurship," but the popular models were based on a charity approach, like Toms shoes: For every pair of shoes bought, another pair is donated to a child in Africa. That is not the answer. Giving people opportunities to create their own well-being is.

It seemed like so many white Americans had the intention of trying to help but were not given the opportunity to truly make a difference. How do you go from being a white savior to an actual ally? What would it look like for Target to truly commit to supporting not just Black charities, but also Black-owned businesses? If these same companies dramatically increased their spending with Black-owned businesses, it could reshape the entire American economic landscape.

That was when it dawned on me: Black Americans make up almost 15 percent of the population—major retailers should commit 15 percent of their shelf space to Black-owned businesses. Period.

The more I thought about it, the more excited I got: If a

company like Target re-allocated the budget for 15 percent of the products that they were buying from corporations like Nestlé and L'Oréal toward purchasing from small Black-owned businesses, it would change the system, uplift all communities, and benefit *all* parties, including consumers.

I decided to post something on my Instagram page—just to get the conversation started. I took out a blank piece of paper and wrote: *Here's one thing you can do for us.*

I knew some friends would think the idea of asking every retailer to pledge 15 percent of their shelf space to Black-owned businesses was an impossible task. And others would say it was not nearly enough; they would want to tear the whole system down. I knew I could wait for someone else to figure this out, or I could begin that process myself by making a clear ask. This was my form of protest.

Just then I heard my buzzer.

Eric McNeal, my good friend and a fashion stylist for Brother Vellies, was on my stoop.

"Do you want to come to the march?" he asked.

"Not in the mood," I said, resigned that my flock would have to go it alone for now. "But I do want to bounce something off you."

We went onto my back patio, which was awash in blooming wisteria, and I showed him the post I had been drafting. I knew it was controversial, and Eric was a good barometer. He is a beautiful dark-skinned Black man who was born and raised in Brooklyn. He has both a lighthearted laugh and a keenly critical eye, and he knew as well as I did that in New York's fashion circles, calling people out was not considered the thing to do.

In truth, posting this ask made me incredibly uncomfortable. But after seeing all the injustice around me, I could not let my fear silence me. And I could not waste my own privilege of having a seat at the table stop me from asking others who were sitting with me tough questions. It was time for companies to prove to me and my community that we do indeed matter.

I watched Eric's face as his eyes tracked every word I had written, line by line, until he stopped, looked up at me steely-eyed, and said with conviction, "Sounds good to me, sis."

Right before I hit publish, I texted June, my agent at the time, and said, "Hey, will you hold @15percentpledge on Instagram as a handle just in case this idea I have takes off?"

I had a hunch it might.

My post started with that handwritten note, and then prompted people to swipe to the following slides, which I had frantically typed out over the previous hour in the Notes section on my iPhone.

@wholefoods @target @shopmedmen @walmart @saks @sephora @netaporter @barnesandnoble @homedepot I am asking you to commit to buying 15% of your products from Black-owned businesses. So many of your businesses are built on Black spending power. So many of your stores are set up in Black communities. So many of your sponsored posts are seen on Black feeds. This is the least you can do for us. We represent 15% of the population and we need to represent 15% of your shelf space.

SWIPE

Whole Foods if you were to sign on to this pledge, it could immediately drive much needed support to Black farmers. Banks will be forced to take them seriously because they will be walking in with major purchase orders from Whole Foods. Investors for the very first time will start actively seeking them out. Small businesses can turn into bigger ones. Real investment will start happening in Black businesses which will subsequently be paid forward into our Black communities.

SWIPE.

Don't get me wrong, I understand the complexities of this request. I am a business woman. I have sold millions of dollars of product over the years at a business I started with $3,500 at a flea market. So, I am telling you we can get this figured out. This is an opportunity. It is your opportunity to get on the right side of this.

So, for all of the "what can we do to help?" questions out there, this is my personal answer. #15PercentPledge.

And then I hit publish.

19

Seeds become trees

Afterward, I put my phone away and went to Kerby's house for dinner. I was in a Covid pod with him, his friend Zoya, Eric, and my friend Elaine Welteroth. None of them said anything to me about my post. But I was glad I had gotten my ask out there. My resolution was to make clear asks. So I did.

It was important to me that I did it for myself. I could have bounced the idea off a bunch of friends before posting, but sometimes lightning in a bottle loses its potency once everyone takes a sip.

At the end of the night, Zoya pulled me aside and said, "I saw your post. I think it is really smart. It took guts."

The next morning, I woke up to a dozen texts and hundreds of comments and DMs. The post was resonating. As I was reading the feedback, a text dropped down from the top of my screen and took my breath away. It was from a friend involved in the Women's March. Someone had forwarded her an email saying that the Proud Boys had a list of Black-owned businesses in New York that they were targeting if any looting happened as a result of the protests: One of them was Brother Vellies.

Within ten minutes, I was on my way to the store. The streets were eerily silent, which added to the ominous feeling I had. As soon as I went in, I started pulling shoes off the sales floor and carefully placing them in boxes. I thought the more barren the store looked, the less likely someone would want to target it. The raffia camp dress that I made for the Met Gala was on display, as were rows of shoes and bags, each a token of the blood, sweat, and tears I had poured into this business over the last seven years. They were now potentially under attack.

It dawned on me that the looting was not being done by protestors, as reported, but more likely by opportunistic people intent on stealing and allowing the Black Lives Matter protestors to take the blame. And, even more sinister, the Proud Boys. I continued to run bags and boxes into the back, I was determined to not let them win.

I piled the shoeboxes neatly in rows and said a tiny prayer: I hoped I would return to this space soon to find it looking exactly as I'd left it. "Tree of Life" by Aretha Franklin played on the speakers overhead. I turned her down and, hands shaking, clicked the lights off and locked the door. It was the first time I felt unsafe in my own city.

As I was making my way back home, Ben Rabb, Brother Vellies' web designer, reached out: He wanted to know if I wanted a website for the Fifteen Percent Pledge idea.

I had not thought of it until that very moment.

"Yes!" I said.

I then texted my friend Mona Chalabi, who does brilliant data visualizations, and asked her to distill the data around Black-owned businesses in a way that was visually digestible for people. She did not even hesitate before saying, "On it!"

The feedback I got within twenty-four hours was overwhelmingly positive. People were excited to see a task assigned to major retailers that could have a positive impact on Black entrepreneurs and businesses. The connection between racial justice and Black-owned businesses was not part of the dialogue in any way at that time. The biggest complaint I got was from some people who said this was racist—that shelf space should go to the best brands, not just Black brands. My argument was that right now shelf space was not going to the best brands; it was going to the most well-funded or well-connected brands. It was much more likely that a major retailer was going to buy another product from Lipton than take a chance on a brand like Brooklyn Tea.

Other folks wondered if there were enough Black-owned businesses to make the Pledge's proposition possible. Even some of my close friends felt that way, which I understood. But I had a friend who had been supporting Black businesses for years, and for years, whenever I'd walk around Bed-Stuy with Sinclair, he'd point to different shops and announce, "Black owned, Black owned." They were usually small stores thriving in their own neighborhoods on the strength of excellent products and community camaraderie. He always reminded me, pre-pandemic, why it was important to support local Black-owned businesses as well. And I understood that I now needed to make this very basic understanding the main focus of this ask.

By Sunday afternoon, celebrities like Reese Witherspoon, Vanessa Hudgens, Megan Rapinoe, Jessica Alba, and Erykah Badu shared the post and explained why they thought it was important to their followers. My flock was getting bigger and noisier by the minute. At the same time, friends and colleagues reached out through different channels offering help: Selby had left *Vogue* by then to become a VP at Snapchat. Her text said, "This is great. Who are we talking to next to get this done? Let's try to schedule calls."

Sophia Amoruso also got in touch, as did Rachelle Hruska, the media entrepreneur and founder of Lingua Franca. Jenne Lombardo, the creator of MADE at Milk, and the designer Rebecca Minkoff sent notes offering to help start a database of Black-owned businesses. I immediately put all five of them in a group text. I knew that the first thing we needed was a comprehensive list so people would know where to shop, and retailers could start understanding the market. These ladies were my secret Charlie's Angels: They helped get the Pledge off the ground. They were all white women, and this was intentional because I knew my Black friends were exhausted. Many of them did not have the emotional capacity to have these arduous conversations at this moment. And most of these white women have never had to have them at all.

On Monday, Sophia introduced me to James Higa, who had worked closely with Steve Jobs for much of his twenty-five years at Apple. His organization, Philanthropic Ventures Foundation, helps people launch and incubate nonprofits. I decided to officially call the organization the Fifteen Percent Pledge and launched our website that same day, which included a petition that people could sign asking major retailers to commit to the Pledge.

Most people had not yet made the connection between Black-owned businesses and racial justice. I realized that they could not understand the financial implications of systemic racism on Black entrepreneurs until we really started hitting them with data. So Mona created graphics to help illustrate the most pressing issues to share on @15percentpledge, like:

1. 42% of Black-owned businesses don't think they'll survive the pandemic.
2. Just 1% of Black business owners successfully receive a bank loan their first year.
3. Black Americans own 2% of all U.S. businesses with employees compared to white Americans who own 81%.

Launching the Pledge had nothing to do with quick fixes or easy how-to steps. It had to do with my desire to give the world the opportunity to validate Black women's work, first and foremost. To be honest, it was incredibly uncomfortable to make that first post because I knew a lot of people at the companies I had tagged. I did not feel like I was calling them out; I was calling them in. I tagged companies I believed could do this and would do a good job and would create impact. It is easier to sit quietly at the table than to flip it on its side. Tagging Sephora was especially risky as I had been working with them for about three years on a collaboration to make travel makeup bags in Mexico. I hoped it would be Brother Vellies' foray into beauty products. The following Monday, I was on our office Zoom daily check-in, when an employee said: "There goes our collaboration."

It was not that she disagreed with the post, it was more that she imagined there'd be blowback. This was a tough one, as I had spent many years making sure that everything was zipped up properly. To go rogue was risky. But my community was also at risk, and there were too many people who could potentially stand to make big gains if the Pledge worked. I felt it was worth it.

On Tuesday, less than seventy-two hours after my post, Blakeley Vaughn, Sephora's senior director of external communications, and the person who agreed to sponsor the very first Brother Vellies show during the Fashion Fund, called.

"What exactly are you asking us to do?" she said, a hint of urgency in her voice.

This was a strange time. Every morning, I was waking up and waiting for either Dr. Anthony Fauci or then Governor Andrew Cuomo to tell me how to go forward with my day. I was still letting packages wait outside for forty-eight hours before wiping them down with Clorox in order to bring them safely into my house. Adding this very big ask to people I was already working with was intense. But I also knew it was necessary—and an opportunity.

I explained my thoughts on the intersection between racial and economic justice, how you could not have one without the other.

"Black entrepreneurs do not just happen to be 'under-represented,'" I said calmly and with compassion. "We have been historically excluded. And Sephora, like every major re-tailer in this country, is guilty."

I heard her sharp inhale. This was not an easy conversation.

"We are all responsible for upholding a corporate structure that is inherently racist," I continued. "Blakeley, you are guilty. And I am too."

In her silence, I could sense that she was carefully consider-ing my every word.

"We are all guilty, but ultimately, the system is to blame," I added. "And this is our opportunity to begin rewiring it for the better."

"I'm listening," she said. I could feel the wheels turning.

"There is a huge and obvious demand in the consumer mar-ket," I explained. "I believe that Sephora should carry the best beauty products possible, and right now you are not. It is easier for retailers to buy from huge conglomerates than it is to take a chance on a new brand founded by a person who looks nothing like the profile of a successful entrepreneur the media has painted for us. People of color want to be able to come into your store and buy products made by people who look like us and therefore understand us. This is not just the right thing to do, I can promise you it is also phenomenal business."

"Where would we even begin?" she finally asked.

"Take stock," I said, my heart racing. This conversation

could have gone a myriad of ways, but Blakeley seemed to understand the proposition. "How many products does Sephora carry that are made by a Black-owned business?"

"We can get that number," she said.

We then discussed all the ways in which to apply that 15 percent number beyond products: How many Black people are on your board? In your C-suite? Work at the retail level? And how do those numbers compare to your marketing? I had already begun tracking how often retailers over-index in marketing: They can boast that 40 percent of the models in their advertising campaigns are Black or POC, and yet, if their true decision-makers (corporate staff, buyers, etc.) make up less than 5 percent, that is optical allyship.

She and I volleyed back and forth all the possible numbers to investigate.

"I get it," she said. "Let me gather numbers. I will be in touch."

Following my call with Blakeley, I realized that there needed to be another public post explaining how to even begin to do this work—whether you owned a large corporation or a very small business. I had been flooded with texts, emails, and DMs from retailers, big and small, wanting to know how they could participate, and I was scheduling over a dozen calls a day, many in tandem with Selby. I realized getting the key information out there was paramount, and I wanted to empower people to start doing the work.

I also knew that, given my bandwidth, I was probably only

going to be able to help the largest companies that had the potential to make the most impact. But if we were transparent about our work together, it would provide a road map for others to follow.

On June 3, I made a second post that read:

Black-owned businesses are the heart and soul of our communities, and they are closing right before our eyes at a rapid pace. They are the most vulnerable and have received the least amount of economic support. All while businesses like Whole Foods, Target, and Walmart thrive. Economic Equality means enacting real change. Taking the @15percentpledge is ONE thing retailers can do to help.

I am calling on businesses of all sorts and consumers to look at this economic pledge in three parts:

One: Auditing and taking stock of where you are at. Look at your existing shelves, hangers, boardrooms, and receipts. How many Black-owned businesses are you buying? How many Black women are in your C-Suite? Do that work.

Two: Take ownership of where you're at—ideally publicly. Maybe only 2% of your staff is black, 1% of your content, whatever it is just own it. Accept it. Take accountability.

Three: Commit to growth. What is your strategy to get to a minimum of 15% and how do you plan to be held accountable?

I am not saying this is easy. I'm saying this is necessary.

. . .

That evening, at 5:34 P.M., I got a text that read:

"Hey Aurora: It is Jenn Hyman from Rent the Runway. I just sent you our RTR audit and goals. Take a look and let me know what you think. We hope it makes you proud."

I had never met Jenn, so this was a terrific surprise.

"Hi, Jenn!" I replied. "I am very excited about this. Can we talk this evening? Also, are you okay with me sharing the work you did internally? I want everyone working with me to see how incredible this is."

She wrote back immediately: "Yes for both."

Embarrassingly, I didn't know much about the company until I started doing research to prepare for our call—and I was floored: Rent the Runway was the fifth-largest purchaser of clothing in America, and Jenn was the co-founder and CEO of the billion-dollar company. She also single-handedly supported a lot of the fashion businesses she worked with while providing a service to women who could not afford to buy those clothes themselves, or who liked the idea of a sustainable, shared wardrobe. We got on the phone that night, and in the days that followed, we devised a strategy to get to 15 percent.

"This week, I talked to dozens of my employees one-on-one," she reported on our second call. "Some of them had horrible things to say about their experiences talking to customers who call in." People on customer service lines, at every retailer and major corporation across this country, are often subjected to racially or culturally loaded attacks. In corporate culture, "the customer is always right" approach can prevail over the experience of human beings at the call centers, which means the employee is rarely empowered to simply hang up the phone.

Jenn also learned that people of color within her organization noted the lack of diversity among the designers the company offered.

"I learned that we are falling short," she said. "Aurora, this is the best thing I've done—shut up and listen. It was a deeply emotional and personal thing for everyone."

I had never met Jenn, but immediately recognized a kindred spirit. She was also the first CEO I encountered who admitted that she didn't know how to talk about race in a boardroom, that she never had to. But this would become a theme in my conversations, as almost every CEO said the same thing.

"I'm not sure that I've ever actually said 'Black people' in a board meeting," Jenn said. "And I don't think I am alone."

To do this work, language is essential. Race is an incredibly complex issue in America that we have not been given the tools to unpack, so we wind up using overly simplistic vocabulary to discuss extremely complicated and nuanced issues. I credit my relationship with my grandmother for my ability to have conversations with people who are defensive or ignorant or simply inexperienced. I understand that a lot of this is determined by how you were raised and how you think about the world. There are not enough conversations happening around race in the first place, so there has been little opportunity for people to practice, which makes talking about big picture issues uncomfortable, let alone the nitty-gritty details. And given the overarching fear about "cancellation," CEOs are often terrified to make a wrong move and suffer blowback. That leads to a failure to launch and paralysis, the worst move of all. What we all must realize about change is that stumbling is evidence of momentum.

Not every CEO was as receptive as Jenn. Some companies said they did not have that many Black customers, so I would remind people that the majority of Brother Vellies' customers weren't necessarily Black. You don't have to be Black to shop from Black-owned brands. I also shared our petition that we asked people to sign in support of our 15 percent requests. In one week, a hundred thousand people had signed. "Here are your customers," I'd say. We were even able to map them by geolocation, so I could prove this wasn't just a coastal thing. This was a country thing.

But the most common defensive response was that there weren't enough Black-owned businesses. So to prove them wrong, and to grow our database, we began a crowdsourcing initiative with Instagram posts that read: "Tag your favorite Black-owned businesses."

People continued to call and text me, wanting to help, including a woman whose handle was @skjelse, a Brother Vellies customer. She offered to organize volunteers to scour the shelves of retailers, both physically and virtually, for Black-owned businesses. I knew most retailers were not even close to 15 percent. The question was, how far did they have to go to make it to that number? But never in my wildest dreams did I imagine we'd see figures as low as what we found.

I started by asking her to do an inventory of Shopbop's Black-owned businesses.

She wrote back, "ON IT."

Another bird in my growing flock.

I posted on Instagram stories, "A volunteer is working on the @shopbop numbers. They have a lot of brands, we need to determine how many, if any, are Black. Please msg her directly so you guys can do this together. WHITE WOMEN, please consider taking this on."

It was challenging in the beginning to decipher what companies were Black owned; a lot of brands are fronted by a Black celebrity but not actually owned by them. Typically these are licensing deals, and celebrities are paid to be the face of the brand, with very little or no ownership in return. Our metric to qualify as "Black owned" meant 51 percent or more ownership. "Black partnered" meant if two or three friends started a business, at least one person was Black (30 to 50 percent ownership). "Black founded" was classified as brands originally founded by Black people who had taken a lot of investment and significantly diluted their equity, or had subsequently sold them, such as SheaMoisture. And while each was important, we knew that focusing on "Black-owned" brands would be the most beneficial for the Black community. Looking further down the road, I wanted to ensure that investors saw value in helping Black founders hold on to the majority of their business, which had not historically been the case.

She wrote within an hour to say "volunteers rolling in." I worried she might get overwhelmed and told her I would take down the post at any point. Or, I added, "we could use it as an opportunity to assign people to Saks, Net-a-Porter, Moda Operandi, Matchesfashion, and Goop." "I like the second idea," she replied. "Making tabs on the spreadsheet for each brand. I will let you know if it is too much, but I have a bit of time on my hands and this feels like a good use of it."

By the end of the week, we had tallies on almost a dozen retailers. The volunteers were a mix of people across the country with no common denominator other than a desire to help, doing crucial work: researching websites, looking at every single brand that a company offered, and then figuring out how many of them were Black owned, versus founded, partnered, or fronted. Some, I learned, worked at the corporate level of the retailers we were investigating.

"Angels are everywhere," @skjelse wrote me in a text.

She was mine.

Ten days after I launched the Pledge, I got on a Zoom with a dozen people from Sephora who wanted to discuss what it would entail for the company to take the Pledge. Blakeley was on, as were Artemis Patrick, the chief merchandising officer, and a few other senior leaders. They had been tracking all the posts I made and had questions.

"Where you are sitting in this exact moment in time affords you the power to change the course of history," I said. "We are all humans above and beyond whatever job we have right now. Sephora is one of the most influential retailers in the world. What you do, others will follow."

We began that conversation by discussing the barriers to entry that have made it next to impossible for Sephora to work with more Black-owned businesses. One example I shared was how different brands had to pay for display placement on the end of the aisles, and each cost thousands per store.

"Who can afford that?" I asked. "Not someone without access to capital."

I could see nods of agreement and the lightbulbs going on around our virtual table.

"We are all in the most privileged places right now to even be on this call," I explained. "You guys have so much influence. Probably more than you ever even realized. And this is our opportunity to get on the right side of this. To be brave and make the first move toward a proposition that could fundamentally reshape the American economic landscape in this century. None of us will ever forget this year, 2020. We will be talking about it for the rest of our lives. We will be talking to our kids about it, answering their questions: What did you do? What do you want to be able to say? We have an opportunity to turn things around. We have a chance to change this country."

That was when Artemis, their CMO, said, "We are going to do this together, right?"

"One hundred percent," I said.

Then it dawned on me.

"I just want you guys to take a moment and acknowledge that it's only women on this call."

I looked around that virtual room at the women's faces, square by square, all calling in from home, where we had been for over thirteen weeks now. I don't think there was a dry eye on that call.

Artemis said, "We're in."

. . .

On June 10, I posted the following on Instagram:

What a difference a week makes. ♥ A little over a week ago,
I wrote an Instagram post and called on 4 of the biggest retailers in America to commit to the #15PercentPledge. That
idea quickly became a movement and an entire organization. And now today, we are thrilled to announce that, of
the four businesses we named, @Sephora is the first to take
the Pledge. With unparalleled influence and power, not
only in the beauty industry but in retail at large, Sephora is
making a historic contribution to the fight against systemic
racism, economic inequality, and discrimination by taking
this Pledge. We commend their early leadership and look
forward to working with them on their accountability and
commitment as we join together in the mission to put billions back into the Black community.

Meanwhile, our Black-owned businesses database was growing and growing—and the dismal retail representation numbers
were coming in from our volunteer flock. On June 7, @skjelse
sent me an update: "We are 86% done (with the Shopbop inventory). Black owned is an enraging (but not surprising) 1.2%.
Will report when final numbers are in."

They came in later that evening. "FINAL COUNT: Of the
937 brands that Shopbop carries, 14 of them are Black owned.
1.4%." One of those fourteen brands was Brother Vellies.

While I had actively chosen to withdraw myself from much of the wholesale landscape, it was still jarring to say that Brother Vellies was one of the most widely distributed Black-owned businesses in the world.

She added that volunteers had already gotten started doing this work for the other retailers we discussed. A hundred women across this country were part of our anonymous volunteer task force—none of whom I've ever met. One of them was clearly established in the retail world, as she looped me into an email with Pete Nordstrom, the president of and heir to the legendary department store. That spurred another conversation, which started with this post:

July 1: "Hey @Nordstrom 👋 You say you are 'committed to change' but less than 1% of your shelf space is Black-owned. We counted only 21 out of the 2,365 brands you carry."

I already had been in touch with Olivia Kim, the woman who had first introduced me to the Okpos and who was the first employee at Opening Ceremony, who was now the vice president of creative projects and home for the Seattle-based department store. She is a forward-thinking woman of color, and I guessed that she had been fighting the good fight for a long time. Sometimes people like her just need some outsized outside support. She flew the idea of joining the Pledge up the flagpole and it worked: With the help of Emma Grede, Nordstrom signed a ten-year contract a year later, in July 2022.

Meanwhile, MedMen had reached out to me in early June. They are the largest cannabis retailer in America, but their stores are only in California, which means, per the law, they can only source their suppliers from that state. I knew this one would be complicated, and heavy. Most of the cannabis companies in the United States are run by white men while thousands of Black people are behind bars for basically doing the same thing. I tagged MedMen in that first post for this reason: It felt hugely important to me to figure out how to bring equity into this space. I thought about Manoly, and also how easily I could have been arrested for selling drugs when I was in college. When MedMen reached out, I started doing research on the complex cannabis industry.

I needed to talk to someone who knew that world more intimately. A friend of mine, Hannah Bronfman, suggested that I talk with her brother Benjamin, as he had worked in what was referred to as "alternative medicine" for about a decade. I had also previously met their mother, Sherry Bronfman, a brilliant Black artist, philanthropist, and activist. Their father's family is Jewish and founded Seagram. When we talked, Ben was very thoughtful about the parallels between alcohol and cannabis and, as a half-Black person, infuriated by the inequities that plagued the industry.

That phone call led to dinner. It was clear he understood why the Pledge was so important. He also runs a fund to help start-up cannabis companies and was a founding partner in a carbon-capture company called Global Thermostat, so he knew the venture capital space, and how difficult it was for Black entrepreneurs to get support. Ben was a real champion—and wanted to help for all the right reasons. He was also in awe of what we had been able to pull off already.

That June, MedMen became the fourth company to take the Pledge. We knew that in California, at that time, it would be challenging for them to get to 15 percent, but they committed to doing the work to help the existing Black-owned brands grow and succeed in order to thoughtfully make their way to 15 percent.

The Pledge is not a crash diet—it is a lifestyle change. The goal is not to get to fifteen by any means necessary. It must be sustainable, which means people must be thoughtful. Company leaders must make a strategy for how to support each and every business they bring on board, especially if those companies don't have adequate resources for production or marketing. The question then becomes: How do you support them and still meet your own requirements?

The brilliance of the Pledge is that it seems like such a straightforward proposition, but once you start to unpack the why and the how, you start getting into deeper issues. Ultimately, those issues are the threads that have woven together this system of inequality for so long. Issues like a lack of diversity on the corporate level, which usually happens as a result of unconscious biases that have to be actively unlearned. It's about peeling back the layers of a fraught system to uncover where we went wrong and then course correct.

In reality, it is very difficult to get to a healthy 15 percent on your shelf space. If you're Neiman Marcus and have had the same buyers working for you for twenty years, it leaves very little space for different or more innovative points of view. Those buyers are more likely to keep ordering Tory Burch flats, products they know will give them a good return. They aren't interested in taking the perceived risk of buying Pyer Moss sneakers—and in many ways they are not incentivized to do so. They have no space to fail.

On top of that, customers are programmed to buy what they see on celebrities who are programmed to wear what is picked for them by stylists who are programmed by the major brands that pay them. Who has the most money to pay to control this narrative? There is a reason Dolce & Gabbana can say horrible things and still be on the body of your favorite celebrity the very next week. That reason is money.

For every meeting that led to a commitment, I spent hours on the phone with many companies who seemed paralyzed. In one conversation Selby, myself, and Elaine, who helped out in the early days of the Pledge, had with the CMO at a major retailer, she said, "Ultimately, I can't do this because I'm afraid we're going to fail."

I responded, "You are already failing. Taking a step toward positive change is always a win, regardless of your pace. Your failure to launch is the fail."

Data was key to proving the main proposition: that supporting Black-owned businesses means everyone wins. We needed to show companies how and why this works, what the consumer demand was, and how the Pledge was a completely different proposition for each company that signed on.

By our one-year anniversary, 385 Black-owned businesses were now on the shelves of the 28 companies that took the Pledge, which had created a pipeline worth over ten billion dollars directed to Black-owned businesses. Taking the Pledge makes smart business sense for companies, as 55 percent of all Americans supported the Black Lives Matter movement and the largest group that cares about these issues are people under the age of thirty-five with an average income of $150,000. They published a report for the Pledge called "Introducing the 15% Pledge, Reimagining the Role of Retail" with all of these findings, including the fact that 79 percent of consumers will end relationships with companies they regard as racist. In short, the Pledge is positive for everyone involved.

When I sat down to write the Fifteen Percent Pledge, it was because I had to clearly ask for what I needed. And I wanted the world to answer positively. But for every win we have had, there have been great losses too. For every retailer that has said yes, there have been others who forced us through uncomfortable conversations only to say no. There have been other opportunities and personal commitments with retailers that I couldn't follow through on because it would've been a conflict of interest. I had to cancel a contract to become the ambassador of a large beauty brand because they weren't taking the Pledge. I knew it would detract from everything I was trying to do at the time if I announced I was the face of a company that would not commit. Part of the responsibility of having privilege means knowing when to pass on the opportunity to take more. Instead, I kept focused on the big picture, which has been my strategy all along.

20

a seat at the table

That summer, in addition to running Brother Vellies (which was growing exponentially), I found myself building what would end up being one of the fastest-growing nonprofit organizations in America. I also became one of the judges for the CFDA/Vogue Fashion Fund. Anna and Steven had asked me to do it in November 2019; then the pandemic happened, so it was postponed until spring 2021. Hundreds of designers applied, and we asked thirty-five to submit formal applications. I was humbled and excited to be one of the ten judges arguing about who should proceed to the final ten.

There was a heated debate for the last spot: An actress turned designer of a sustainable brand or a soft-spoken Black designer who had used his life's savings to move to L.A. from Atlanta and was running his business out of his apartment despite having dressed Kamala Harris for her inauguration.

I believed that lesser-known designer fully deserved it. He was incredibly talented but did not have the same access the others did. Some of the judges argued that his sales volumes were not that high, and his materials weren't as glossy and put together. I believed that was a resource issue, and not about talent. I also thought back to 2015 and wondered, "Who at this table spoke up for me?"

This was a moment where I knew that I needed to speak up for what I believed was right—otherwise I was still a part of the problem. I was reminded of what my mom said to me when I won the Fashion Fund: "I hope you no longer feel the need to compete in systems that were not designed for you."

Now I think about designers who don't get into the Fashion Fund: It doesn't mean that they are any less brilliant than the ones who do. It just means they may be brilliant in a different way. They may be building their own new system.

Tom Ford was one of the judges on the panel that year and he had graciously invited me to be his guest at the Met Gala, which had also been postponed due to Covid. It usually happens in May, but in 2021, it took place in September.

In July, I got a call from a director at *Vogue*.

"We were thinking it would be really amazing if you could dress AOC for the Met Gala this year," she said.

My jaw dropped and my heart skipped several beats at the same moment. I'd only ever made dresses for myself, so I told her how incredibly honored I was for the opportunity and asked if I could have a couple of days to get back to her. That was not what any editor traditionally loved to hear but I needed time to consider if I could make it happen in a meaningful way. This was the end of July. Ben and I had started dating by then and were supposed to be going away; I was finally getting a vacation, my first since launching the Pledge. Plus, I was writing this book! We had also just moved to Los Angeles for a while. Since that Proud Boys scare, I had received many nasty comments on Instagram plus unsettling, aggressive messages in my DMs and via email. I'd also received several death threats. I began getting nervous that people were going to show up at my door in Bed-Stuy. It was made clear to me the people making these threats knew where I lived.

With so much going on, I wanted to call around to figure out if I would even be able to get something like this done before I emailed back to say yes. There was no explanation about what they had in mind other than the theme that year: "In America: A Lexicon of Fashion." I had free rein.

My first question was: Why does AOC want to go to the Met? She is the most famous progressive in America if not the world. How is the Met Gala relevant to her or her message?

Another part of me wondered if she would even show up. Every designer has a story about making the dress of their dreams for someone to wear to a high-profile event, only to have the person cancel at the last minute. In my estimation, it seemed likely that the congresswoman would be called into a more pressing way to spend her second Monday in September.

Nonetheless, I started to come up with ideas for dresses and sent some early sketches to her team. The feedback was, "Go bigger, go bolder, this is a special moment for her."

I reviewed all the dated protocols on how to dress a congresswoman: closed toe, covered shoulder, certain length. One of the first questions I asked her team was if she was comfortable with an open-toed shoe. They responded, "Absolutely!"

Originally, I thought I would put her in a suit, but she wanted a dress.

I spent weeks sketching different ideas. I kept thinking that people were going to criticize her for attending an event like this. But I believed she could be elegant and glam and beautiful and still show up with a message that was authentically her. That gave me an idea: What if we wrote that message on the Brother Vellies Nile bag she would be carrying? Or even on the back of her dress? Something that was very AOC. I looked at some of the slogans she had used historically, like "Change takes courage" and "I am not running from the left, I am running from the bottom."

The more I contemplated her core platform, the more I believed that it was important to use this as an opportunity for her to deliver her message. We mocked up a bunch of slogans.

I was looking for something that made sense for this particular moment. And then I heard a clip of her saying, "Tax the rich," which was something she and other congresspeople had been debating that very summer. I paused: This would be a roomful of people who needed to hear that message. You could wear that on a pin to the mall or a party with your friend and no one would say anything to you. If you showed up to the Met Gala in a room with the richest, most influential people in America, that would be a different situation. Some of the people I knew she needed to bring that message to the most might be there.

The most important thing I've learned in my life is that you need to be yourself in every room. And I wanted to make sure that Alexandria could be herself at the Met Gala and that perhaps she could also use her dress to be the Trojan horse to deliver a message to such a powerful and privileged room.

I Facetimed my design assistant and said, "I need you to write something on the back of this dress." He started to play around, writing in big bold letters using an Apple Pencil and iPad.

I had no idea if AOC would go for it. I knew some people would not get it or would hate it. So the questions were: Are there enough people who are going to be affected, inspired, motivated, or influenced by it in a positive way to counter any negativity? Will this garner enough conversation to bring the topic onto a broader stage? Will her supporters understand her intention? I thought, "The Metropolitan Museum has invited us, these two women of color, to an institutionalized event that's been historically frequented by people who are at the apex of white privilege and multi-generational wealth." Anna knew what she was doing. She knew we would show up with something to say. I was still nervous.

Alexandria and I met in New York for a fitting, where I showed her the "Tax the Rich" sketch.

She looked at me with a sparkle in her eye. "I love it."

One of the women we asked to work on the dress was born and raised in the Bronx. She gasped when she saw it. She then looked at both of us with glassy eyes and said, "This is the most important thing I've worked on in my whole life."

We settled on white for the dress itself. The color felt peaceful, and we had gathered bolts of material and fabric thoughtfully. When my design assistants, the patternmaker, and I went back to have her try it on, we were all so nervous. We had only hammered out the design on Thursday night and the event was Monday. Most designers spend months doing this. At the fitting, as she slipped on the dress the room was silent. She looked at herself in the mirror and then she turned around to see the back of the dress in her reflection.

Her eyes narrowed and focused on the text reading word for word how it spilled across her back until her eyes darted up at mine through the reflection. "This feels dangerous," she said. "I love it."

Something that is so striking about AOC is her size: She is so petite, but simultaneously so threatening to the status quo. It amazed me how a human could occupy such a small amount of physical space on the planet but have such a huge effect on the world.

During that fitting, she told me that she used to come home from her waitressing job and watch the Fashion Fund on TV. "When you won, I was like, 'OMG that girl did that?'" she said. "I was so proud of you!"

I was reminded of the geese formation: Sometimes that V is so wide that you don't know who is flying with you.

Two days before the event, I got a call from Anna's office asking if Ben wanted to join me at the gala. I knew how many people were cut from the list that year, and there were a million people she could've given that invite to who would've paid six figures. Looking back now, I think she was worried about me.

I said yes.

We got dressed at the Carlyle. I was also dressing the CEO of Gap Inc., and several other guests were wearing Brother Vellies shoes. That meant that I was running around, making sure everyone had what they needed to feel their best. Paper Puerto Rican national flowers adorned AOC's red Brother Vellies strappy stilettos. She wore hoop earrings, an ode to the Bronx. To some degree, I wanted the dress to fade away, so the message was the focus.

As we waited for our car to come, I could tell that she was nervous. We all were. Her current fiancé, then boyfriend, Riley, arrived with Ben. They would be our escorts for the evening, which took a bit of the pressure off. But it was hot, and we were running late.

When we finally walked the red carpet, people were craning their necks, looking for Rihanna, so they barely paid attention to us. Since the message was on the back of her dress, we practiced how she would stand for photos, her back turned, her face peering over her shoulder, so people would have a hard time running photos without the message.

Once inside, I saw Diane von Furstenberg and introduced her to the congresswoman.

"You made this dress?" Diane said.

I nodded and AOC did a spin to turn around.

"*You* made *this* dress?" she said emphatically. "I love it."

I have always thought of Diane as one of my fairy godmothers; she has been so supportive of me. That night was no exception.

As we made our way through the crowd to dinner, I heard

some people ask, "Is that Demi Lovato?" Others, who'd figured out it was AOC, were in awe.

After dinner, we inadvertently walked in on Gigi and Bella Hadid doing an Instagram video with other big models that *Vogue* would likely use on their social media footage of the evening. I was so happy when they invited the congresswoman to have her own glam moment, which she did beautifully, with a spin. Everyone was in awe. This tiny, beautiful woman was being unapologetically bold.

We started walking through the hallways of the Met when several of the waitstaff took notice of us. At these events, the servers are supposed to be discreet, but that did not stop several from making their way over to us.

"I'm from the Bronx too!" one woman said, dressed in her uniform, smiling so wide her eyes were squinting. "It is so good to see you here."

"Representing!" another man said under his breath as we walked by.

I realized at that moment that she was there for them, not the people sitting at the tables. She was there for the people who had been showing up at every job across the country for the past two years, continuing to make this world spin while those with privilege were able to stay home or go attend a gala. She wanted people to pay more taxes, yes, but what she really wanted was for the everyday person to be supported.

In that way, the Pledge's ask is similar.

As the night came to an end, we began making our way to the exit when we heard a rumbling outside. As we grew closer, we could decipher that it was a crowd chanting, "Tax the rich! Tax the rich!"

While we were inside, images of AOC in our dress had been circulating on social media and the message had spread like wildfire. Her followers had shown up in droves to support her and spread the message so that everyone could hear it—including some of the men inside who needed to hear it the most.

AOC got the same sparkle back in her eye that she had when she first saw the design. She ran toward the crowd and started yelling back: "I love you!"

The next morning, I woke up to my phone ringing. My publicist was calling to inform me that *Good Morning America* and CNN both urgently wanted me on that day. I thought back to the event and felt good about what we had done. From my perspective as a designer, I wish I'd had more time with the dress itself, to construct it. But overall, AOC looked beautiful, she had a great time, and she stayed consistent to who she is, which meant wearing her values on her sleeve. As a designer that is all you can really hope for.

Later that morning, my mom sent a text, "Nice dress!"

That made me smile—of course, she got it immediately.

Then Republicans, on Fox News and Twitter, started mocking AOC's choice to go to the Met Gala, where the tickets can cost thirty-five thousand dollars. Trump's family members piled on. That was when the narrative shifted. That started fueling darkness. I did a CNN interview where they changed the crawler to DESIGNER AURORA JAMES RESPONDS TO BACKLASH. AOC's team were not fazed by the negative feedback from Republicans, though they were happy when President Biden held a news conference where he talked specifically about increasing taxes on the ultra-rich. A dress at the Met Gala was sparking conversation across America. This was the power of fashion, as my mother had taught me.

That Sunday, I was at Little Dom's, my favorite place to eat in L.A., with Ben and one of my favorite people, his son, Ikhyd. We had just ordered the blueberry pancakes when my phone started buzzing with every other bite. That was how I learned that AOC and I were on the front page of the *New York Post*. My inbox was full of queries from right-wing publications trying to get info about my childhood, my tax records, and even my abortions. I was asked, "We have an understanding that there were multiple appointments that needed to be made at gynecologists. Do you have any comments?"

Anna emailed and apologized that they were trying to come after me personally. She reiterated that what I did was really brave. Other friends argued that making the front page meant it worked and that any press is good press. But I didn't feel that way at all: The home that I had bought with my own money, as a refuge, was now being positioned in the media as a lavish purchase made with my boyfriend. And worse, people were using reverse image searches to locate my home address. Some of the tax payments I could not afford to pay in order to make payroll in my earliest years in business were now being used to make me out as a grifter. Some of the most difficult decisions I had to make over the years as a woman and a founder who was dedicated to supporting other women were now being weaponized against me. I was heartbroken.

Most of all, I was worried I would lose my community's trust: People believe what they read. It also proved to me how upset people could get when two women of color dared make a statement that challenged the status quo. I had a nonprofit organization and a brand that supports artisans that I needed to protect. My home address had been leaked and I simply wanted it to end. I now have a whole new level of respect for Alexandria, fully understanding the level of ridicule and scrutiny she deals with every day.

But what no one acknowledged was that AOC was one of only three women to wear a Black female designer on the carpet at the Met Gala. The other was Chirlane McCray, Mayor Bill de Blasio's wife, who wore a dress by Fe Noel, as did Jackie Aina. This was the biggest fashion event in New York just sixteen months after the murder of George Floyd. Almost every celebrity in that room had posted a black square after his death and committed to doing better, but which of them had? Which of their stylists had even pulled dresses from Black designers as options? Few were even wearing American designers. For all the talk about how people are changing, supporting, advocating, you have to see who actually shows up.

21

Joyful Rebellion

I was outside of the Bowery Hotel when I received a text message from Steven Kolb: "Congratulations, Aurora, you're getting the Founder's Award this year!"

I called him immediately: "Steven, after all these years, you're going to text me one of the most important things you've ever told me in my life!"

He laughed and said, "I'm sorry, I thought you were busy!"

"Never too busy for that!" I responded.

Eleanor Lambert was the founder of the CFDA and the first person to activate designers to come together as a group to strengthen American fashion and create a community. The CFDA has always felt like a family to me. I didn't know anyone in fashion when I was starting, and the designers I met through the CFDA became my friends. Getting the Founder's Award, which is for people who have had a large impact on the industry and the world, was poignant. So was the fact that Steven said the board had voted unanimously to present me with the award that year.

In the days leading up to the event, I had to request who I wanted to present the award to me. I did not hesitate: Anna Wintour. I knew this was a huge ask. I also knew that she was someone who had, in her own way, been a fierce advocate of me and my work.

She agreed.

Anna also asked me once: "Are you going to be an activist? Or a designer?"

"Respectfully," I responded, "I think I can be both."

I was thinking about this exchange as I took my seat at the table the night of the CFDA Awards, where I was about to be bestowed the coveted Founder's Award. It had only been two months since the Met Gala and while things had simmered down, the whiplash of that event really confirmed for me that both are possible. And in certain climates, both may become completely necessary.

This was the first time I was reunited with the rest of my CFDA design community since the pandemic. The event was at the Seagram Building and it felt like a family reunion—Diane von Furstenberg and Steven Kolb were both there, as were Tom Ford, Zendaya, and Eva Chen. There were so many familiar faces in that room and I was struck by how many of them had supported me over the years: Bethann Hardison, Paloma, Liya Kebede from lemlem, and Precious Lee, one of my favorite and earliest Brother Vellies models, who is now experiencing a long-deserved meteoric rise in her career, were all sitting at my table. Ben sat next to me, beaming. Iman was across from me. I was already feeling emotional—and then Anna took the podium.

As I watched this petite woman, an emblem of American fashion in a custom Prada red floral dress, I thought of all the ways that she had been used to personify everything the world lamented about fashion: critiques about young models, Kate Moss's weight, fur coats, and the lack of representation. It also made me realize how we spend so much time in life trying to point blame at a "who" when often it is really the "what."

The Anna that I had come to know was funny, charming, discerning, and thoughtful. She was also a provocateur, and a risk-taker: By selecting me to win the CFDA/Vogue Fashion Fund, she made a bet on me, not just to the tune of three hundred thousand dollars, but it was also well documented that no company that had ever won the Fashion Fund had gone out of business. The win always felt like more than money, especially since at the time, many other fashion editors would not even respond to my emails.

I also knew that Anna was one of the largest fundraisers for the Democratic Party. She was the first person many of us turned to the day Trump became president. She was a persistent organizer and rallied people in a way that was unusual to see. She also gave many of us courage. On this evening, she made me think of AOC: both women whose physical size is incongruous with their power.

Anna had her speech written out and as she read from it, I noticed that her voice was a bit shaky. I realized that she was emotional, as well. She started by saying the first time we met, I forewarned her that I was "a crier." That got a laugh from everyone who knows me. But then she went on to say, "Aurora does not spill her tears because of nerves or fears or frustration. They are part of her empathetic makeup, something that is as true to her as her unwavering ambition to make the world a better place."

By then, my heart was in my throat. Anna went on to speak about the Fifteen Percent Pledge in ways that deeply moved me—she described it as "industry transforming, life changing, and era defining." I had only just finished writing my speech, there at the table, scribbled on note cards. Until the moment when she was getting up on the stage, the idea that I was receiving the Founder's Award felt too surreal for me to even contemplate my words.

We locked eyes as I took the podium. I swallowed the lump in my throat, looked at my notes, and then I told the Pledge's origin story—starting with the phone call with a friend that sparked my idea and the Instagram post that followed. I then highlighted all the milestones that we had hit as an organization thus far, such as:

- Twenty-nine of the largest and most influential companies across the world had signed the Pledge.
- Through contractual commitments with our Pledge Takers, more than ten billion dollars was being shifted to Black-owned businesses.
- Since launching, more than six hundred Black-owned businesses had been placed on the shelves of our Pledge Takers.

- Many Pledge Takers were not only tracking and improving their Black shelf space, but their BIPOC-owned business numbers were improving as well.

My favorite fact was that the Fifteen Percent Pledge was the largest economic driver for Black American entrepreneurs that this country has ever seen. The most daunting was that we were also one of the fastest-growing nonprofits in the country.

I spoke about how I launched Brother Vellies with $3,500 at the Hester Street Fair, grew it to a company that sold millions of dollars of products, and almost went under due to an exploitative financial relationship. I looked up and locked eyes with Carly Cushnie, another incredibly talented Black female designer, who had lost her business during the pandemic in an eerily similar manner. I went on to share how I learned that my journey as an entrepreneur paralleled the experiences of so many Black founders—specifically that investors never wanted to invest in *me*. Although that should come as no surprise given that only forty-eight Black women in this country had ever been able to raise more than one million dollars in venture capital—an unfathomable fact. Imagine the value I have been able to drive for my community with Brother Vellies and subsequently the Pledge on the strength of just $3,500 and a $300,000 grant. Imagine how much more I would have been able to do this whole time had I been properly resourced.

When we don't empower the smartest, most inventive people in the world, regardless of their color, we are the ones that miss out. It is entirely possible that this world has already both born and lost a person who, had they been empowered and resourced, would have helped cure cancer, or end world hunger, or solve climate change. I believe that our society has a duty to give everyone in this country the opportunity to be their best. We as a people have too much at stake to not allow all of our children the chance to blossom and give us back their gifts.

That night I told the audience that I had been working toward launching an investment fund called Friends and Family. While this was separate from the Fifteen Percent Pledge, as that organization cannot finance businesses, it was related in that the fund would focus on helping Black-owned companies secure loans or investments. I wanted to be the investor I had always longed for myself. I also knew that access to capital would quickly become one of the largest barriers to entry for Black-owned businesses to be able to meet the demands that the Fifteen Percent Pledge was asking businesses and retailers to make possible. And we needed to start working on solutions for that issue.

Ben had begun introducing me to several venture capital and private equity funds, many of whom declared their commitments to DEI but had never invested in Black-owned businesses and had no Black people on their management teams. After meeting many of these men myself, I could say confidently that I would probably not have been comfortable taking money from any of these firms for Brother Vellies, so I did not feel comfortable referring them to any other Black founders either. In my search for suitable partners, several people mentioned Alisa Williams, a Black woman at the Silicon Valley–based private equity fund VMG Partners, which had invested in some of the most successful Black consumer packaged good brands, like the Honey Pot, a plant-based feminine care product company;

Briogeo, a brand that focuses on hair care; and the skin care company Shani Darden.

When I met with Alisa in Los Angeles, I was enamored: She was incredibly smart and pragmatic. From the minute we met, I felt a deep value alignment. Back home, I went to send her an email to say how much I enjoyed meeting her and found a note from her that she had sent two days after I had posted about the Pledge back in May 2020. It was one of thousands of emails I had received, so rediscovering it now, in this context, was poignant. She wrote, "Dear Aurora, I am an investor and I work with a lot of Black brands and retailers. This is precisely what this country needs. Let me know how I can support you."

I got goosebumps and thought of my flock: wings flapping, all working confidently in their own way, powering this work forward with their combined currents. We have been working together ever since with an early allocation of $25 million to invest in Black entrepreneurs. Our next raise, for a second fund, will be for $200 million.

Because of my own lived experience, one of my core focuses right now is helping Black entrepreneurs get over and through many of the financial obstacles that arise when you are scaling a business. One startling statistic I learned was that it costs a Black woman, on average, $125,000 more to start a business than a white woman. So many early-stage businesses raise money through peer groups and family members—so what happens if your family does not have that kind of money? Or, if you have been working in retail for all these years to support your family, and don't have significant savings? I had my own experiences to compare this to.

Working on the Pledge made me realize how vital data is. I knew, from the beginning, that I had to back up what I knew to be true about the inequity in business. I would need statistics. For so long inequality and the Black American experience has been largely anecdotal. Gathering data around the true realities for many Black entrepreneurs has confirmed what we have long known and felt. The data grounds the argument. Black people do not happen to be underrepresented: They have been historically and systemically excluded. People are so resistant to seeing how these systems are set up specifically to exclude Black people from succeeding—and how this has nothing to do with talent and everything to do with access to resources.

By this point, the Pledge had grown to over a dozen women committed to advocating for Black-owned businesses and helping major corporations restructure to become more inclusive holistically. With each new Pledge Taker, the hypothesis that this was good business for everyone involved was being proven. We knew that in order to keep adding new retailers and organizations, we had to keep growing our own organization. This was why our extraordinary executive director, LaToya Williams-Belfort, and our chairwoman, Emma Grede, both called me to make a proclamation: We needed to host an event to raise funds and more awareness for the organization. They suggested a gala, but I was hesitant.

As someone who blushes at the idea of hosting my own birthday party, the idea of hosting a large-scale fancy fundraiser felt terrifying. At the same time, I knew that Black creatives, entrepreneurs, and professionals along with our allies deserved a moment to celebrate and be celebrated. I also knew that the important work we were doing needed to be funded so we could continue to pay the team we already had in place and expand it even more. I thought back to the Met Galas I had attended, most recently with AOC, where the dress broadcast such a loud message. This time, I wanted the message to be different. I wanted the dress code to be "Black Tie, Black Designer."

The PR firm that was working on the event thought it was a great idea—and asked me to put together a list of Black designers with hyperlinks to their websites so people would know where to shop.

"That defeats the purpose," I said.

At a certain point, I wanted to turn things around on us, the consumers. It is important that we hold ourselves as accountable as the retailers. Ultimately, we can get as many Black-owned brands as possible onto shelves, but if the consumers are not buying them, the retailers will not be able to sustain the proposition. In the same way that we hold the power to make this change happen, the power is also in our hands to see it through. Presented with the opportunity to be able to shop Black, we must buy Black—and in this instance, wear Black.

I also wanted people to go to their favorite stores and ask which Black designers they carried. If the answer was, "Um, none," to then ask, "Why?"

Possible answers might include: They are hard to find. There are not that many. I would not even know where to look.

All the answers point to why the Pledge is so necessary. But I wanted people to do their own discovering—I was not going to send hyperlinks.

Once the dress code was settled, we focused on the honor-
ees: Iman was our easy first pick. She had started her namesake
cosmetic line for women of color in 1994, which opened doors
for so many entrepreneurs like me. She received the Pioneer
Award. Stacey Abrams was given the Inspiration Award as a testament to her work, which was clearly changing the landscape
of democracy in the United States. We sent invitations to all
our Pledge Takers, many of whom bought tables, which meant
I got to see Blakeley from Sephora in real life for the first time
since that game-changing Zoom. When we hugged each other,
Blakeley burst into tears.

Desiree Rogers was also there, as the former social secretary
to the Obamas had recently resurrected Fashion Fair, a historic
Black-owned cosmetic brand that Sephora was championing.
Ron Robinson, a cosmetic chemist who'd spent over a decade at
Estée Lauder before finally making the leap to launch his own
brand, BeautyStat, came, as did Tamron Hall, who has her own
talk show and loved hearing all these stories of entrepreneurs
who were growing their business as a result of the Pledge. Lauren Santo Domingo and Natalie Massenet were both there,
women who had revolutionized the luxury e-commerce space
through founding Moda Operandi and Net-a-Porter, respec-
tively.

We held the gala at the New York Public Library and the
beautiful room was packed with people who had also, over the
course of the two years since the Pledge launched, helped it become the fastest-growing nonprofit in the country. Selby, who
was now on our board, was at my table that evening. Emma
Grede, our chairwoman and instrumental in bringing Nord-

strom on board with a ten-year contract, hosted her own table. Eva Chen was there on behalf of Instagram, who had given us a donation in support of the event. Mosha Lundström Halbert, a Canadian editor and a good friend, helped to sign up Hudson's Bay, Indigo, and Sephora Canada, all of whom had committed to our Canadian adoption of the Pledge, which meant 15 percent of their shelf space being allocated to BIPOC entrepreneurs. Dapper Dan, Rosario Dawson, Dominque Jackson from *Pose*. And of course everyone took the dress code seriously. It felt like I was a flower in the most glorious garden. So many beautiful looks, and so many included Brother Vellies shoes!

I now understand that Brother Vellies and the Pledge are a manifestation of the same exercise: recognizing underrepresented groups that have been historically exploited, and then creating opportunity to share their work in the spaces they deserve to be boldly occupying. The question for me has always been: How can you be a catalyst for all of that in a way that is disarming to the system and detractors—and actually make the change feel joyful instead of threatening?

Not only do the companies get to share all these incredible products—whether beauty or fashion or spirits or (fill in the blank with literally any industry)—but they will make money too. Plus, the individual employees who work at these corporations get to feel a larger sense of purpose at their jobs every day. Belonging and productivity are part of solving the problem. This is not a charitable proposition. We are doing good business.

Quite often people will kindly offer to introduce me to a major retailer who has yet to take the Pledge. My response is always, "Thank you, but please don't." I am not trying to convince anyone to do the right thing and do good business. If they don't want to get on board, they can age themselves out of relevance and become the dinosaurs that they are.

I am not responsible for forcing corporations to change what they do not want to. And besides, there are days you ask questions and days you get answers. If a company is unwilling to take the Pledge and commit to Black people and our allies in that way, as a consumer, I would prefer to know. I can then take my dollars elsewhere.

Fifteen percent is not too much to ask.

A year after Sephora signed the Pledge, I was on a call with the company founders in their accelerator program, all women of color. That had never happened before. And every single one of them was amazing. One was a twenty-four-year-old woman named Olamide, who owned a brand called Topicals. She shared that it had sold out in a day and a half—faster than any brand in Sephora's history. I had never even heard of the company. She is now raising her Series A funding at a valuation of $100 million. Sephora is thrilled to carry her and realized that they had been missing a spot in the market.

Sephora also introduced me to Danessa Myricks, a talented professional makeup artist who created a color cosmetic brand to make tones and shades that are truly diverse. I had heard that her line was really taking off at Sephora and her own direct-to-consumer channels. Unlike the Rihannas and Pat McGraths of the world, who entered Sephora with large teams and financing behind them, Danessa was a two-person show, and her business was flourishing in a way that was incredible to watch.

I had heard that she was considering raising capital so she could take her business to the next level and I was excited to talk to her. As soon as we got on the phone, she told me about her decade-long journey, putting up booths at trade shows and building her community, which turned into the loyal following that got her to where she is now—a critical junction for her brand.

Talking to her was like talking to another version of myself.

She told me that as a makeup artist—who was also a dark-skinned Black woman—she always had to be able to work with all skin tones. So she started playing with layering, color, and formulations in a unique way to create a brand for all skin tones and types. That is the magic with Black makeup artists and hairstylists: They have no choice but to always know how to do *everyone's* makeup or hair. The default in the beauty world is white, so they are forced to innovate if they want something that will work for them.

After she told me about building her business, I could sense that she was beginning to let her guard down. At one point, she laughed.

"I can't tell you how relieved I am to be on the phone with someone who has a shared experience," she said.

"I feel the same!" I said. I intuitively understood her experience, and wanted to be for her what I had been looking for in the early days of Brother Vellies.

But working with Danessa Myricks is in no way a charity proposition. It is an incredibly smart business move. In the same way that Sephora carrying her brand is an incredibly smart business move. In the same way that shopping from her and allowing your dollars to funnel into the Black community is an incredibly smart move—for anyone who wants to live in a place that feels more fair, more bountiful for all.

While I was never able to raise helpful capital for Brother Vellies, I was able to grow a business and in turn create ten billion dollars in revenue opportunity for my investors, for women of color, and for my colleagues, who have long supported me in this journey.

In the end, we didn't need them to believe in us. We believed in ourselves.

I believe there is no such thing as Black Girl Magic. This is a story of a Black woman's hard work. My love, my passion, my frustrations. My highs and my lows. My mistakes, my wins, and an ode to the path forward that creates opportunity for all of us: Black, white, or otherwise. I believe you are either part of the problem or part of the solution.

The sun is accessible to all of us, we share it equally. Use her light to bloom in unexpected places. I am here. You are here. We are all together. And the only way for any of us to get through is to not forget that. You made it here, to the end. You're in my V formation and we're flying the distance.

And I have to tell you, we're just getting started.

My mom has often said, "Life is a relay. You have to know when to catch the baton and when to pass it on and how to work together so that when you ultimately arrive at the finish line, you don't end up alone."

afterword

I t's all very emotional.

Our paths to get to where we want to go are never linear. And it's so tempting to get hung up on the seemingly insurmountable roadblocks along the way. But when we find ourselves there, staring up at the fortress, feeling overwhelmed by the size of the wall, we instead must look next to us, at the other people who are there as well. And then realize that we can scale that wall together. Or tear it down.

If you've gotten this far in my story, I am sure you have questions. I do too. Simply put, my brilliant, beautiful, intelligent mother and I remain very close from afar, but far from close. Its imperfect, it's a season, and it's the space I need to heal. I'm still on that journey and so is she. We are girls and then women before we are ever mothers, and that is okay.

A few days ago, I was officially voted in as a vice chair of the Council of Fashion Designers of America. Holding that title means a lot to me. As a designer, I have gone through almost every CFDA program and that first grant from the CFDA/Vogue Fashion Fund was part of what helped me get here today. I love the fashion industry, but I will also be the first to tell you that it has a lot of work to do. We need to create an ecosystem that fosters American design talent more; we need the large American designers to invest back into the next generations. Otherwise we will continue to see a design industry that is possible for only a handful.

Just last month, after a final year of stretching myself and my business to its fullest capacity, I was finally able to pay off Bart. I would be lying if I didn't tell you it was incredibly, incredibly hard. What started as an earnest attempt to cover a single purchase order for seventy thousand dollars, ballooned to me paying off over a million dollars. So now, for the first time since 2016, Brother Vellies will be free from his grip, just in time for our ten-year anniversary. I'm not mad, because I've learned so much from that experience—about the inequities that exist in business, how great something can look on the outside while suffering on the inside, and how much you must truly love what you're doing in order to have the stamina to continue in this dance of entrepreneurship. And I chose to spend more money in order to not have to sign an NDA so that I could tell this very story and share in my learnings. These are the investments we make in one another. Sometimes we win, sometimes we lose, but we must try. We must invest in each other.

This is the ethos that drives me, and the Fifteen Percent Pledge. As of summer 2022, two years after I inadvertently launched a global movement with an Instagram post, twenty-nine companies have taken the Pledge, starting with Sephora. As a result, we are now in the process of shifting over $10 billion in annual revenue to Black-owned businesses. Three thousand Black-owned businesses are now registered with our Business Equity Community—and 90 percent of them are women led.

In less than two years.

Over the past year, we have done a deep dive with McKinsey & Company to figure out which companies are the most important to focus on getting to take the Pledge moving forward. And what we learned is that if Target, Walmart, Amazon, Kroger, and CVS commit to the Fifteen Percent Pledge, we could generate $1.4 trillion into the Black community by 2030. And I believe this can happen.

People often ask me if I have reached out to them, or if I would like an introduction to someone they know there. The reality is this: Every major retailer across this country is aware of the Fifteen Percent Pledge. They are aware that the consumer landscape is changing. And that more and more customers want to be able to shop diversely and ethically. Companies have to want to change. They have to want to make a commitment that they are ready to be held accountable for, in partnership with Black women.

Target launched a campaign—Black Beyond Measure—which appeared to be in defense to the Pledge. I don't want to disparage any of the work they have done; they work with many Black founders whom I know and love, and some of the work they have done is fantastic. In many ways they feel like they are Pledge Takers by proxy, because they've been forced to run this race with us and keep up. More so, my question to them is: What are you afraid of? Why not boldly tell all of your customers that you stand with us and truly commit to trying to get from the less than 2 percent that you currently hold to the north star goal of 15 percent shelf space? That means sharing your purchase orders with us to make sure your terms are truly helpful. That means being open to suggestions of Black brands that may not know the inroads to your shelves. That means being part of a collective of businesses, from retailers to financial institutions to tech companies, that realize closing the racial wealth gap in this country will take *all* of us putting our heads down and actually doing the work. And the best work is never done in silos.

In the early days of the Pledge, James Higa told me that the quickest strategy people employ to kill movements is to silo the activists and changemakers from one another. No matter what the small differences we may have with one another on the ways we want to get to the destination, it is most important that we acknowledge our shared visions for the future.

At the end of the day, no one person, organization, or corporation will be able to solve these issues alone.

It will take community.

It will take all hands on deck.

All stars in alignment.

And all birds flying together to that final destination of parity.

acknowledgments

There have been so many of you flying alongside me in this V formation over the past several years. It is not lost on me how tough the terrain has been at times. How much we've had to push one another. How different the landscape has looked in certain moments from what we expected. We have gone the distance. And while sometimes the road ahead still seems so far away, I want to remind all of us to take the time to look back and truly acknowledge that we've come so much further than we probably ever felt possible. Perhaps because we've done it together.

I want to thank my mom, whose life has been so hard, for giving me the space to tell my story without being given the full space to tell her own. Mom, I love you. You have done an incredible job. I would not be here without you.

Nanny, I love you. Dad, you too.

To my book family, Marya, Libby, Liz, I am endlessly grateful for your patience, thoughtfulness, and belief in my story. For helping me get it onto the page in a way that my incredibly high bar manages to actually feel great about. Gillian Blake, Yang, Chris, and Sebastian Kim, thank you for supporting me to make it physically beautiful as well.

Thank you to Darnell Strom and my UTA Family.

Rachna, Bryn, and KCD. Janna and BR. Steven, Leigh, Thom, and the CFDA. And everyone else who has had a hand in supporting me while I supported this book.

Countless artisans across South Africa, Kenya, Morocco, Ethiopia, Namibia, Haiti, Mali, Bali, Burkina Faso, Ghana, Nigeria, Italy, Mexico, and the United States have been a part of Brother Vellies. Thank you to all of you for your incredible talent and for inspiring me to keep this little engine going, despite how terribly hard it has been at times. Thank you to all of my staff at Brother Vellies, then and now, for hanging in there with me too. It really means the world. Truly.

Thank you to Liza and Raz and my Hoffman family for giving me exactly what I needed to start 2020 and make the big ask.

And as it pertains to that ask:

I will always hold a special place in my heart for some of the people who jumped on so quickly to not only acknowledge it but help make it happen: Selby Drummond, Ben Rabb, James Higa, Mosha Lundstrom, Sophia, Rachelle, Rebecca, KJW, Eva, Jené, June, Jill, Elaine, Jordan, Eric, Gavin, Marissa. Mike and Josh. Ben.

LaToya and Emma.

To Blakeley and Artemis—thank you for saying YES. I will never forget that day for the rest of my life. You are so brave. Look at what you did.

To the twenty-nine (and counting) major corporations who have taken the Pledge:

Sephora, Rent the Runway, West Elm, *Vogue*, Yelp, Med-Men, Indigo, Macy's, Bloomingdale's, Bluemercury, *InStyle*, Madewell, CB2, Crate & Barrel, Crate & Kids, Gap, Old Navy, Athleta, Banana Republic, Kith, Next, Moda Operandi, Hudson's Bay, Sephora Canada, Matches, JCrew, Ulta, Nordstrom, and Victoria's Secret.

To the men in the different chapters of my life who let this book be about me and not us.

And to Ikhyd, who let me become your bonus parent over the swirl of the past three years. I am so honored to be in your space and in your life. I cannot wait to see the man you will grow up to be. I love you.

Mr Chow. Mia, Sade, Andie, Virge, Darren, Alisa Williams, Mike Mauzé and Brandon Maxwell, Behnaz, Kyle Hagler, Rishi.

To everyone on social, you don't know this, but you've talked me off a ledge, you've picked me up when I thought I couldn't run anymore, you've given me the courage to keep fighting, the confidence to say no. The confidence to say YES. You've empowered me to ask questions of the people who have never been questioned. And you've fought for me in times when I didn't have it in me to keep fighting. You have never let me down.

And I couldn't have done it without you.

Let's stay wild. And bloom wherever we want to. Unapologetically.

Wildflower

AURORA JAMES

Discussion Questions

1. Early in Aurora James's life, her mother comes across as a fiery, independent woman. But when Winston enters the picture, that all seems to change. How does this affect James's upbringing and her relationship with her mother?

2. Talk about James's teenage rebellious streak—including its consequences. Why do you think she acted out, and why was it so pivotal to who she's ultimately become?

3. What were the inequities James saw in modeling? How do they inform the work she does today?

4. James observes that "hurt people hurt people" when examining her own relationship with her mother and the abuse inflicted by her stepfather. How can understanding the origins of generational trauma help heal us?

5. What insights into the fashion industry surprised you, particularly for up-and-coming designers? What were the ways in which James worked to build a company and empower creators within a system that can be restrictive? How much does access—or lack of access—to funding influence the success of emerging entrepreneurs, especially entrepreneurs of color in America?

6. How do James's values align with her talents? What about her passion inspires you?

7. "The best type of fashion, I believe, are those items that tell that person's story." What story does your sense of style tell about you?

8. James travels to Morocco, Nigeria, Namibia, South Africa, and Kenya. What insight into these African countries does she offer, especially when it comes to fashion? What did you learn about the local artisans and how white Westerners perceive them? What Western ideologies can you identify that, while well intentioned, have actually been harmful?

9. How conscious are you of where your dollars go when you purchase an article of clothing? Will reading James's memoir and learning about the Fifteen Percent Pledge change how you shop? Why or why not?

10. Do you believe that there is a benefit to changing a system from the inside out? Are there certain systems that need to be completely done away with? How was James able to make the most change to the fashion world—by working within the system or working to change it?

11. The Fifteen Percent Pledge aims to help companies do what they do best for communities that have been historically excluded. In which ways are Brother Vellies and the Fifteen Percent Pledge similar exercises? How can we use our own strengths in day-to-day life to promote equity?

12. How celebrities, influencers, and other public figures use their platforms varies dramatically. What, if any, responsibility do you feel people with a platform have to advocate for causes, issues, or marginalized groups?

13. James came to the United States at age twenty-three and launched Brother Vellies at a flea market just a few years later. How do you define the "American Dream" today? Is James's a story about the American Dream?

14. Black women are the fastest-growing group of entrepreneurs in America. What might explain this growth? How can initiatives like the Fifteen Percent Pledge play a role in this?

15. Lack of access to non-predatory capital is a theme in James's entrepreneurial journey. How large of a factor do you feel capital access is to the success of emerging entrepreneurs? How heavily has this affected people of color in America who have not had the opportunity to build generational wealth in their families?

PHOTO: SEBASTIAN KIM

Aurora James is the creative director and founder of the luxury accessories brand Brother Vellies and founder of the Fifteen Percent Pledge, an initiative that urges retail giants to commit 15 percent of their shelf space to Black-owned businesses by creating clear business strategies and attainable goals. A Toronto native, James lives in Brooklyn and Laurel Canyon.

aurorajames.com
Instagram: @aurorajames